Life Before Noon

The Guy's Little Black Book For Success After College

Life Before Noon

The Guy's Little Black Book For Success After College

Dan Gura
David deMontmollin

FIRST U.S. EDITION 2010

ISBN 1449587402

EAN-13 9781449587406

Library of Congress Cataloging-in-Publication data is available.

Published in the United States by Dan Gura and David deMontmollin, Tampa, Florida.

Edited by Jamie Pilarczyk

Cover design by Chasity Hageman

A work of College State of Mind, LLC.

www.collegestateofmind.com

10 9 8 7 6 5 4 3 2 1

PRINTED IN THE UNITED STATES OF AMERICA

Syllabus

How To Use This Book

How To Use This Book

You don't realize it now, but there is life before noon. You have spent the last years crawling out of bed at 12 p.m., while the world has been cranking since 7 a.m. To be successful after college, you need to adapt.

Every time you hear the phrase "real world" do you wonder what the hell people are talking about? Life in college is just as "real" as life after college. This book explains how similar both phases of your life are. Fear of the unknown is going to be present during any transition in your life, but rest assured, you are better prepared than you think.

The academic side of college obviously plays an important role in graduation, but what is often overlooked is the social evolution that one goes through while in college. You might not think it now, but late night keggers and early morning tailgates have helped you develop important social skills. The ability to meet new people and interact in different social environments will make you successful regardless of what career you decide to pursue. Earning your degree shows that you are intelligent, but what good is a 4.0 GPA if you can't hold a conversation with a co-worker?

This book was written for guys who partied their way through college by guys who partied their way through college. It was written as casually as a conversation while bellied up at the bar. Hard work in the classroom is essential, but the lessons learned outside of it are what will make you successful from this point forward. We chose the 10 most challenging obstacles that you will encounter and broke them down into 10 easy-to-read lessons. Pursue them in order or skip around as you please. Just know this, reading this book will put you ahead of the competition and onto the fast track to success.

Life after college isn't difficult; it just starts before noon.

For more lessons and tips, please visit www.collegestateofmind.com.

SENIOR YEAR
THE FINAL COUNTDOWN TO GRADUATION

Now is the time to take some important steps that will pay off big time once you graduate. There is more to do than just finishing your senior year and putting on a cap and gown. Learn how to optimize your schedule for future employment. There are also a few things to check on that will be the deciding factor in your future employment.

- ✓ Lesson 1: Staying In School Longer May Be A Viable Option
- ✓ Lesson 2: Optimize Your Class Schedule
- ✓ Lesson 3: Minor In Something, Anything
- ✓ Lesson 4: Grad School, The Perfect Fall-Back Option
- ✓ Lesson 5: Boost Your GPA The Easy Way
- ✓ Lesson 6: Start The Job Process Sooner Than Later
- ✓ Lesson 7: Use Your Professors For Job Leads
- ✓ Lesson 8: Your Classmates Have A Wealth Of Information
- ✓ Lesson 9: Get a Part-Time Job That Builds Your Resume
- ✓ Lesson 10: See What Internships Can Lead To A Career

Staying In School Longer May Be A Viable Option

We know you love the title of this lesson. Don't get us wrong, we don't want you to slack off and fail a class just to stay in school. We do want you to understand that life in college is awesome, and you should savor every minute of it. You are never going to be in that type of environment again.

When you are in college, expectations are low. Not much is asked of you. If you want to stay up all night and sleep all day, nobody is going to think you are a loser. If you don't shave for a week and wear the same shirt every day, nobody is going to think you are a slob. You can pretty much do what ever you want while you are in college.

You are about to transition into life after college and things are going to be great. Why not continue the college fun if the opportunity presents itself? There are plenty of perfectly good, socially acceptable reasons for you to stay in school for another semester or year. In the following lessons, we are going to teach you about all of them.

Now, if you are going to stay in school longer, you need to get in the right mindset. The obvious reasons to stay in school, just to name a few, are keg stands, sorority parties, road trips, drinking games, all-night benders, intramural sports, late night pizza, and random drunk hookups. When you leave college, these things are obviously going to be harder to pull off.

That being said, you can't just throw everything aside and party in your last days. You still need to finish your classes and find a job. But, make the most of your time left while in college.

⬤ **Life Before Noon Tip**

> *Think back to your first couple years in college. What was the most fun? Now, use your short time left to do those things as much as possible.*

◇ Lesson 2 ◇

Optimize Your Class Schedule

As you are setting up your final semesters of college, there are a few steps to take to make your time more valuable. First, don't schedule any Friday classes unless necessary. This gives you a three-day weekend and a work day to make any calls for jobs. Next, schedule the once-a-week, three-hour late classes. You might think that the 6 p.m. to 9 p.m. Thursday class will eat into you social life, but that is not the case. At 9 p.m. you will be pumped to go out and so will other people in the class. It is the only time frame you can ask a girl to get a drink after class. If you can find a girl to grab a drink with you after an 11 a.m. class, never let go of her.

In a perfect world, you have one class per day, Monday through Thursday from 6 p.m. to 9 p.m. The next step is to convince your friends to take the same classes as you. Knowing someone in your class will give you a reliable classmate to compare notes or help out when you miss a class. Most senior level classes also have group projects, so it is always nice to have someone you know in your group instead of all randoms.

Finally, map out the remaining courses you need to take before you graduate. Research which ones offer late classes and how they are going to fit into your schedule. Most colleges keep the same class schedules semester after semester, so if you have two classes that only have a Monday late class, make sure you don't end up having to take both those classes your last semester. Many seniors end up with 8 a.m. classes because they don't have any alternatives.

▶ Life Before Noon Tip

Do some extra research and ask your classmates about the reputation of the professors in your the final semester. You don't want to end up with a professor that rides his students in your last semester of college.

◇ Lesson 3 ◇

Minor In Something, Anything

A minor separates you from the pack of all the other people that are graduating with the same major. For example, a civil engineering degree with a business administration minor sounds a lot more well-rounded than just a civil engineering degree. It gives you the option to go after project management jobs and not just technical ones. Plus, it gives you a better story to tell about yourself and looks good on your resume. Finally, if you are looking to go to a graduate business school, it will show that you already have some of the background necessary.

You may not realize it, but many of the requirements for a minor you probably have already taken as electives in your major. Many minors only require five classes, but most people think it takes a lot more. You might have already taken three of them in your electives for your major; for two more classes, you can get a minor.

Minors are particularly easy to get if you switched majors. You probably already have taken all the classes needed for a minor before you switched. Be sure to check with your advisor and fill out the necessary paperwork.

You can also go for the double minor, which is easy to do with minors that overlap each other. For example, a minor in business administration and a minor in accounting are only two classes different. We know you will be tempted to go for the triple minor, but once you go past double, it will just look strange.

Don't pass up the chance to get a minor. It is easy to do and looks good on your resume.

▶ Life Before Noon Tip

Research all the minors and see which ones match up with your electives.

Grad School,
The Perfect Fall-Back Option

While graduate school may not seem like an option for you, it is a good back up if the job market falls apart. So, if you are about to graduate and have absolutely no job leads, continuing with grad school is a smart option. It is much easier to continue with grad school straight out of undergrad. If you take a semester off and move back home, it will be difficult for you to re-enroll.

There are a couple of great things about grad school. First, people respect grad school and will assume you are intelligent because you were accepted. (It is not as hard to get in as you think.) Second, if you find the perfect job while in grad school, it is OK if you drop out and start your career. Nobody is going to call you a college drop out. Finally, if you end up completing your master's degree, you will be a respected person in your field of work and command a higher salary.

Getting into grad school takes some planning. In some cases, if you miss the admission deadlines you have to wait an entire year to reapply. You have to take the entrance exams, fill out lengthy admission forms and have a minimum GPA.

Don't think you have to go to grad school where you enrolled as an undergrad. Take the opportunity to find cities that you always wanted to move to and then apply to the grad schools in those cities.

▶ Life Before Noon Tip

Research online the admission deadlines for graduate schools.

◇ Lesson 5 ◇

Boost Your GPA The Easy Way

While most employers don't care much about GPAs, there are certain industries that won't even interview you if you don't have the minimum. There is not much difference in a 2.6 and a 2.7, but if you can raise a 2.9 to a 3.0, then it is a smart move. There are two ways to improve your GPA: retake classes you did poorly in or take some easy electives.

If you retake classes it will not only help improve your GPA, but it will also serve as a good refresher for you as you near graduation. So many classes are taken and then the material is forgotten by the time you graduate. It can be very beneficial to re-learn some of the material and get a little extra practice. Be sure to check with an advisor and confirm that you can replace a grade before signing up for the course.

The other way to boost your GPA is to take easy electives in addition to your base schedule. Not only are easy leisure skill classes such as bowling, basketball, Frisbee, golf, tennis, and racquetball guaranteed fun, but you will get some exercise and meet classmates with similar social interests. It is one of the few opportunities to actually enjoy yourself inside of the classroom and still receive a grade. The leisure skill classes fill up quick, so be sure to snag them as soon as you are able to register.

▶ **Life Before Noon Tip**

Talk to your friends about what leisure skill classes they have taken. Write down their favorites and plan on taking them in your last year.

Start The Job Process Sooner Than Later

By junior year you had probably changed majors several times and finally settled on what field you wanted to pursue. How do you envision life after college? Do you want to work for a big multinational corporation or a small business? Do you want a desk job or something that involves being in the field? Do you want to go to the same office each day or are you willing to travel all the time for your job? These are the questions you need to ask yourself before you start looking at job leads.

Think about an industry that will always have demand for your career. It does not have to be on the Fortune 500 list or even the biggest in your city. You need to be in a field that has demand outside one company. That way you always have an option to switch companies if you get passed by on a promotion.

Starting the job process as early as possible provides a great opportunity to establish some leads and find out more about companies. Many times a company manager will want to hire you but won't have a job open. When a job does open he will want to fill it quickly. If you are in his radar from your contact with him prior to employment, you will be the first one he will call.

▶ Life Before Noon Tip

Seriously think about your career and where you envision yourself five or 10 years from now. Write down notes and refer to them as you research companies. Will these companies provide you with a platform to accelerate quickly?

Use Your Professors For Job Leads

Early in your college experience there will be many classes that may not draw much of your interest but are mandatory for all freshmen and sophomores. Most of these classes will be introductory courses and have tons of students in them. It can be a bit intimidating since it is one of your first experiences, and you really don't have any face time with the professor. Once you are into your major, the class sizes will shrink to a respectable size, and the classes become more interactive.

The professors in your major are teaching those courses because they are experts in them. Most college professors worked in their field of study and that is how they gained so much experience. Professors have connections. Get to know your professor and ask him or her for help in lining up a job.

Of course, your professor probably will not be inclined to help if you are a problem in class or have poor attendance. Don't let something so insignificant hinder your chances at landing a job. Employers are always going to give referred applicants a better shot than people they don't know. If you know you want to enter a field similar to your professor's, then be sure to let him know. He can help you develop a specific skill set that will make you successful in that particular field. It also cannot hurt your grade to know your professor on a bit of a personal level and also let them know you are serious about their field of interest.

▶ **Life Before Noon Tip**

Find out one personal fact about each of your professors. If one likes fishing, be sure to mention fishing to him next time you talk. You will get to know them on a more personal level, and they will have more interest in helping you out.

◇ Lesson 8 ◇

Your Classmates Have A Wealth Of Information

Your classmates can be just as good of a resource as professors. These students have decided to major in the same field as you, and their aspirations are no different. Use these students as a resource for answers to questions because they have been going through the same process of interviewing and job hunting. Ask them about particular interviews they have had because no two are exactly the same. Ask them what kinds of questions they had and what some of the answers were that they gave.

Don't make it one-sided. Be sure to give your accounts as well so both of you benefit and can continue to help each other throughout the process. The process also includes graduation because your classmates will be going through that transition as well. It probably won't be easy for you to move back in with your parents, if that is the plan, and it won't be easy for the others either. Ask them questions about how they are going to adjust or why they are moving to a particular city. Ask about getting rid of furniture and cheap ways to accumulate more.

If they have a job lined up they might also be able to recommend you to their employer or point you towards some other companies with which they were interviewing. The bottom line is not to let an opportunity pass by without at least giving it consideration. Whatever job you choose, you will rely heavily on co-workers. So begin networking with your classmates for some good practice.

◆ Life Before Noon Tip

Don't be overly pushy with your classmates. Sometimes there is only one job open with a company, and they don't want the competition. But once they land a job, be all over them if there are any other available positions.

Get A Part-Time Job That Builds Your Resume

Unless you are taking a full class load (at least 15 hours), you should be able to find some part-time work while attending school. Holding a part-time job during school will be more similar to a full-time job than any three-month summer gig. It will also allow you to build your resume with some work experience.

Employers want to know that you were disciplined enough to actually make it through school and earn your degree. If you can show them that you handled a full work load while working part time, you will be a well rounded candidate that handled more than just school.

Not only are part-time jobs going to help your resume, but let's face it, you will be making some cash!!! Plus, it is a great way to meet people off campus. The number one reason for a part-time job is to create a full-time one. Any employer looking to hire who has the chance to try out a part-time student getting ready to graduate will offer him the job over some other applicant 99 percent of the time. Even if they aren't necessarily looking to hire, they can become a great reference.

Don't use the excuse of not having a car as a reason to pass on part-time jobs. Many part-time jobs are also available on campus. On-campus employers are extremely flexible with times and schedules because they know that students are always busy with school. The pay will probably not be great, but it will be easy money with a great schedule.

▶ **Life Before Noon Tip**

Look through the job postings at your college web site. Take a chance and apply for one for which you don't think you are qualified. They are just as desperate in filling the position as you are in getting a job, and many times you will be the only one applying.

◇ **Lesson 10** ◇

See What Internships Can Lead To A Career

Internships are resume builders, not a way to earn money. You should not worry about the pay but more about how it will reflect on your career. Most college students will not have many bills while in college, so this is the best time to see what internships are available.

Most companies offering internships will be flexible with schedules because they know the majority of interns are students. Internships give companies an opportunity to try out different potential candidates with minimal financial obligation. It also gives you a chance to get your foot in the door before graduation comes around and the interviewing process starts. Once graduation commences, all of your peers will be applying for jobs and many will be applying for the same one.

An internship will not only allow the company to give you a try, but it will also allow you to try out the company. As an intern you will be able to find out if you really want to work in a particular industry before making a career commitment. Many people end up hating their jobs but will not make a career move because they are financially committed and don't have the flexibility to look for another job. As an intern, if you don't like a particular industry then you can cut ties at the end of the semester or possibly even sooner.

If scheduling permits, start the internship during second semester of your junior year. This will give you time to experience internships in different industries if you quickly you don't like the first one. If you find you do enjoy the internship, try to set up another one during your senior year. This internship can focus on another aspect of the job, putting you even further ahead of the competition.

▶ **Life Before Noon Tip**

> *Don't even consider pay when deciding on internships. Go through the interview without asking what it pays. Rather, talk about how much you are interested in the field. It will impress them much more than somebody bitching about $10 versus $10.25 per hour.*

$\diamondsuit$ **2** $\diamondsuit$

FRESH START
FIND YOUR BEARINGS IN LIFE

Before you take the road to who you are going to be, you need to take an inner look at yourself. Don't let people tell you about the "real world" because nothing you are doing is "fake." Find out why you may actually enjoy spending time with your parents and how to use your age as an advantage in the work place.

- ✓ Lesson 11: There Is Life Before Noon
- ✓ Lesson 12: You Are Living In The "Real World"
- ✓ Lesson 13: Your Parents Are Actually Smart
- ✓ Lesson 14: At This Age It's OK To Talk To Strangers
- ✓ Lesson 15: Skeletons In The Closet
- ✓ Lesson 16: Relationships, Work, Sleep
- ✓ Lesson 17: Think Before You Jump
- ✓ Lesson 18: Your Learning Has Just Begun
- ✓ Lesson 19: Use Your Age As Motivation
- ✓ Lesson 20: Don't Forget To Breathe

◇ Lesson 11 ◇

There Is Life Before Noon

It may come as some surprise, but you will learn that there is life before noon. While you spent the last four years of your life avoiding 8 a.m. classes and rolling out of bed in the afternoon, in life after college you will spend many waking hours with the morning sun. Basically, the a.m. and p.m. of your productive hours will flip-flop. Instead of planning days around 8 p.m. to 5 a.m. parties, you will plan evenings around your 8 a.m. to 5 p.m. work schedule.

When you have a job and have to wake up early, your priorities will change, but that is it. Instead of partying more and working less, you will be working more and partying less. Don't let anyone tell you that is a bad thing. When you only have so many hours to party, you tend to make the most of them.

You may be thinking to yourself that there is no way you can wake up at 7 a.m. each morning. You know yourself and you know how tired you are at that time. While it may be unthinkable right now, a couple years from now you will actually enjoy waking up early, because it will give you extra time to be productive in your day. Does waking up early mean that you won't be able to party any more? No, but instead of going out at 10 p.m. and closing a bar down, you will hit happy hour right after work and call it a night by 10 p.m. Rest assured you still have the weekends for the occasional balls-to-the-wall, late-night drunken fiesta.

College is a phase of life that you eventually have to leave, but that doesn't mean you have to grow out of it. You learned way too much in college to not take something with you and apply it everyday in and out of work. Once you realize that "life after college" does not have to be different from "life in college," you can concentrate on more important things such as securing a job. The first step in being successful in life after college is accepting that there is life before noon, and you must be part of it.

► Life Before Noon Tip

Make an effort to wake up by 7 a.m. once a week your senior year. This will give you an idea of what your schedule will be like once you start working. NOTE: Setting your alarm for 7 a.m. and hitting snooze again and again until noon does not count!

You Are Living In The "Real World"

Nothing you are doing right now is "fake." Don't let people tell you how things will be in the "real world." Life in college is your real world right now, and everything you are working toward is real.

People use the term "real world" to undermine your accomplishments. High school students say it to grade school students, college students say it to high school students, fathers say it to fathers-to-be, etc., etc. Don't listen to them! Everything you do now and all the knowledge you are accruing will benefit you in the future.

You're not going to go through any drastic changes after graduation. You adjusted from high school to college so there is no reason you won't adjust to life after college. Enjoy your last days of college and embrace the transition. This is an exciting time and not a time to worry. Worry about life and death, not about this.

At this point in your life, you have been through plenty. The next phase of your life will have its own set of experiences that will once again appear to be so difficult. You overcame life's challenges before, so why can't you leap over life's future hurdles?

When you left high school, you were faced with tough challenges such as moving, meeting new people, and leaving your comfort zone. College graduation will present these same challenges but have some confidence in knowing that you have already experienced it, succeeded, and have become stronger for it. Remember that everything you go through is a learning experience that will benefit you later in life. It may not be the exact same, but you can take a little something from each experience and apply it at another point in time.

▶ **Life Before Noon Tip**

Compile a list of challenges you encountered after high school graduation. Now compile a list of expected challenges after college graduation. You will be surprised at how many are the same and how many you have already conquered!

Your Parents Are Actually Smart

Don't get the idea that because you passed some 3000 level statistics class or that you earned your undergraduate degree that you are smarter than your parents. Yes, you may have achieved a higher level of education than them, but that doesn't equate to experience. You will not realize this when you first get out of school and why should you? You thought you knew more than them before you got your degree. Your degree doesn't represent your capacity for life knowledge as much as it does your commitment. Your parents have been through more and have more experience than what you gained in your four (or five, or six...) years of college.

Just because your parents didn't tell you things growing up, doesn't mean they didn't know what was going on. They know more than we will give them credit for because they have been through it. The sooner you realize this the easier it will be to actually admit that your parents are cool and you enjoy being with them. Maybe cool is a bit of a stretch, but your relationship will definitely be better than before.

After graduation, you will begin to understand your parents on an adult level. Your view of them will change. They will no longer be a provider of money (but definitely still accept money as long as they offer). Instead, they will be a provider of advice. We know it sounds pretty lame, but it is true. You will become friends, or closer friends, once you discover that they weren't so full of it all along.

▶ **Life Before Noon Tip**

Start to acknowledge your parents' birthdays with more than a bar shout-out. A card means more than you think, and it shows you have matured.

◇ Lesson 14 ◇

At This Age It's Ok To Talk To Strangers

How many times have you said to yourself, "If I only knew back then what I know now." Why don't people tell you these things beforehand? Usually, the reason is that they are resentful that nobody told them when they were young so they are stubborn and want you to find out the hard way also. Plus, advice from friends is usually not politically correct; therefore they think it is a waste of time to tell you. We were just in your shoes, and we had to learn the hard way. Things would have been much easier if we had the advice that we are giving you in *Life Before Noon*.

It is easier to get life advice from a stranger. This way it is the complete, unfiltered truth and not something catered exactly how you want to hear it. You don't have to make the same mistakes the rest of us did, because we are going to tell you about them. This way it allows you to fast forward your life and choose the path that best fits you.

No two people will transition into life after college the same. There will be obstacles along the way that test you. Be happy to know that it isn't your typical "test," and there isn't just one correct answer. Having a clear game plan will give you the advantage you need to be successful quickly after college. The lessons of this book are essential for all college graduates. It gives you an unbiased look at decisions that are headed your way.

▶ Life Before Noon Tip

List the things that are important to you and let them be a factor in the job selection process.

Skeletons In The Closet

Ok, you messed up big time when you were a freshman. Who cares? Don't let the past define you as a person. If you made some bad decisions in your past, sulking about them does not do anything for your future. The less you ponder your mistakes the sooner they will be erased from your mind and become a distant memory.

No one makes all the right decisions in college. Your decisions thus far must not have been too bad because you were accepted to an institution of higher education, will soon be graduating, or already have a diploma in hand. Use everyday as a learning experience and try not to repeat mistakes. In your career, there are going to be plenty of mistakes and poor decisions made. If you let regrets get to you they will just continue to put you in a hole and affect your future work.

Adversity is something that everyone is going to go through in life. Whether or not you bring it upon yourself is unimportant. It may sound weird to say this, but it is actually a good thing to make mistakes. There is no way to work through adversity if you have never had any. Learn from it, and overcome it. This is going to be one of the most important qualities you will develop.

Overcoming adversity is a major factor in separating leaders from followers. Nothing will ever be perfect all of the time. If you can work through problems and make it seem like all is well so your client or co-worker does not know the difference, then there will be a place for you in any company.

Do not let past mistakes or adversity affect you. Focus on the future, not the past.

📑 **Life Before Noon Tip**

> *Think of someone else who is worse off than you. If nothing else, it will make you feel better about yourself and help you realize things could be worse.*

Relationships, Work, Sleep

If relationships and work take up two-thirds of your life and sleep takes up the other third, then no time is left for you. Don't let this be your life! Relationships and work are both great, and everyone hopes they get to experience both. If you don't have any relationships, sexual or platonic, and have no job, then you are probably not in very good shape. Enjoy work and relationships, and use one as a release for the other. Be passionate about both, but don't let them consume you.

Have something else in your life to give you balance. It could be charity work or a hobby. Sports and exercise are common hobbies that serve as great ways to take your mind off more important things. Whichever one you choose, be sure to commit yourself. If all you do is work for 10 hours a day, spend eight hours with a friend or significant other, and sleep for the other six hours, then you will drive yourself crazy.

Not only are hobbies good for a physical break from everyday life, they also serve as a mental one. It is too easy to let stress affect your work or personal life. People bring personal issues to work and it not only affects their performance, it also affects the performance of their co-workers. Everyone can be affected by the "down" mood.

The same goes for bringing work home. If someone is waiting for you to get off work, they are looking forward to spending time with you and don't want to hear about how awful your day was. Enjoy your time at work and at home knowing that more than each exists. Don't forget about the personal challenges that await you because career decisions overshadow them.

To have a fulfilling life, have something other than work and a relationship.

🏴 **Life Before Noon Tip**

For the other alcohol enthusiasts out there, try taking one drinking game and vary the rules slightly to make it unique. Introduce as many people to this game and see if it circles back to you at any random parties.

Think Before You Jump

No one will deny that there are plenty of challenges for a recent college graduate. The longer it takes to get a job, the more stressful it becomes. Soon you become desperate. Add this on top of the other trying factors you are going through such as relocation and saying goodbye to friends, and you might be ready for a breakdown. While all of this is inevitable, there will be just as many opportunities as challenges available.

No one thinks about the opportunities at first because everything else is so overwhelming. Try to enjoy all of the changes. Be ready for opportunities and think through each option. Sometimes people jump into a situation to relieve stress or they think that nothing better will come along. When everything is so overwhelming, it is hard to contemplate all the options that come your way.

Before you make any big decision, take a step back and ask yourself why it's perfect. Is it because all of your friends are already settled and you feel you are falling behind? Is it because you can't stand living at home anymore and want to get out? Is it because you feel people view you as a slacker? If you answered yes to any of these, then maybe it isn't the best fit.

Whoever said opportunity only knocks once is full of crap. Did you marry the first girl you ever dated? There will be plenty of opportunities to take advantage of, just make sure they are a good fit.

If you do accept a job that isn't right for you, don't be afraid to man-up and move on. Mishaps along the way are not necessarily mistakes. Understand that you discovered ways that things shouldn't be done thus taking one step closer to the correct way. Trust that the right situation will come along.

You will want to begin work soon after graduation to give yourself some financial freedom, but you do not have to accept the first offer you receive. Take life for all you can. Carpe Diem! But think before you jump.

► **Life Before Noon Tip**

> *Try to have three solid job leads during your senior year and have one selected BEFORE you graduate.*

◇ **Lesson 18** ◇

Your Learning Has Just Begun

Graduation is yet another milestone in your young life. It is one accomplishment of many more to come. At one point it probably seemed so far away, but here you are getting ready to begin your career. Be excited for all the opportunities you have had and for all those still waiting for you.

One common misconception about graduation is the thought that education is over. This could not be any less true. Although a classroom may no longer be the forum, you will never stop learning. You will learn that many people put themselves at a disadvantage by refusing to adapt to new technology or by not taking advantage of a learning opportunity. Never stop learning!

After college, one sure way to rise above your co-workers is to take advantage of any courses your employer offers. Your human resources department may offer optional training to employees who choose to become experts in fields that may be slightly outside their every day job functions. Taking these classes will not only help make you a more valuable employee, but it will also show your superiors that you want to excel and take on more responsibility. Put yourself in a situation where you have people at all levels of the hierarchy coming to you for answers.

Life is not going to stop after college so your education shouldn't either. You will always learn things through experience, but don't think that learning a technical skill ends after graduation.

◣ **Life Before Noon Tip**

Find out if your potential employer offers tuition reimbursement for future graduate or continuing education classes.

◇ Lesson 19 ◇

Use Your Age As Motivation

College students are generally in their twenties when they graduate. There will be enough motivation to be successful when you graduate, but there will also be more than enough intimidation. Don't shy away from challenges because you are the "new" guy in the office.

Being in a new environment, learning something new, and feeling that you are officially on your own are just a few intimidating factors. Age is another one that affects too many people. Instead of feeling that you are at a disadvantage because of your age, use it as an advantage. Being young and just out of college will be refreshing to any office. Things are often done without question because that is how they have always been done. Use your uncorrupted views to make fresh decisions. Industries change, and it is important for employees to change with them. You have a wealth of education and eagerness at your disposal.

As important as it is to bring new ideas and ways of thinking to your job, it doesn't mean you should take crazy risks just to prove a point. It can be very beneficial to take a risk as long as it is calculated. Be ready to support your decision whether it is a success or failure. Regardless of how risky you want to be, make sure to at least be involved.

Don't think that your ideas are less valuable because you have less experience. On the same note, don't go into meetings thinking that you know everything. There is a vast difference between cocky and confident.

With all this being said, some co-workers are going to be threatened by you. Prove them wrong by working the hardest. Show your co-workers that you have plenty of good ideas to offer, but you know you still have plenty to learn from them. Remember that learning is not necessarily a lesson in how to do something, but a good lesson in how not to do something.

Being young comes with advantages in the work place. Use them!

▶ Life Before Noon Tip

Think of just one good invention idea or book idea you came up with in college. Why not pursue it on the side and try to make it happen?

Don't Forget To Breathe

The most important thing for college graduates to remember is also the simplest: "Don't forget to breathe." There won't be as much down time as you think so you must always remember to create some.

Challenges in the office aren't anything you can't handle. Work-related projects will be more important than homework assignments, but what you may not realize is that they are probably easier because they tend to be done the same. Each task will differ, but your resources and methods may not. It's not as hard as you think, because you aren't constantly worried about a grade. Your "grade" will be based on results. As long as you produce and make good business decisions, then you will be fine.

There are two important questions to ask yourself before making any decision that will make your job much easier, "Does your decision protect your company's assets?" and "Is your decision in the best interest of the company?" If you can answer yes to both of these questions, then you are making a good decision. If not, then revisit the issue at hand and come to a decision that supports both of these questions.

In your personal life, you may be faced with some tough decisions. Who to date? Spend your money to fix a dent in your car or pay rent? Before you go with the easiest method, take a step back and look at your decision and how it affects you in the long run. Is your current girl friend smothering you? Is having a car without a dent more important then getting evicted?

Don't make things harder than they are. Any issue will be easier to solve if it is broken down and dissected. Work through issues methodically and don't over-think them. New opportunities will, of course, bring new challenges for you to solve. Remember to look at it calmly and know that you have worked through similar challenges before and have already mastered the process.

Remember not to freak out. Most difficult situations aren't that difficult once you think them through.

▶ Life Before Noon Tip

Passing your final, parting ways with friends, and finding a new place to live are all more difficult than starting your career.

◇ **3** ◇

LESSONS LEARNED
CLASS AND WORK ARE MORE SIMILAR THAN YOU THINK

The classroom is much like the business world. That being said, you already know more about the business world than you think. Use the social aspects of dealing with your professors, classmates, and homework in your future jobs when dealing with your boss, co-workers, and work assignments. The lessons learned while having fun in college will be the reason you earn a paycheck after college.

✓ Lesson 21: Your College Search Is Just Like A Job Search
✓ Lesson 22: Attending Class Is Just Like Going To Work
✓ Lesson 23: Your Classmates Are Just Like Co-Workers
✓ Lesson 24: Your Professor Is Just Like A Boss
✓ Lesson 25: Your Classroom Is Just Like An Office
✓ Lesson 26: Your Homework Is Just Like Work Assignments
✓ Lesson 27: Spring Break Is Just Like A Work Vacation
✓ Lesson 28: Throwing A Keg Party Is Just Like Event Planning
✓ Lesson 29: Selling T-Shirts Is Just Like Entrepreneurship
✓ Lesson 30: Going Out to Bars Is Just Like Networking

Your College Search Is Just Like A Job Search

When you were in high school and thinking about which college to attend, you made a list. The list was based on schools that you wouldn't mind going to and probably a couple that your parents preferred. You filled out an application to each college, visited most, talked to people you knew attended the school, and researched every aspect of what the college could do for you. You didn't get accepted to every college you applied to and ultimately chose a college from the ones that accepted you and that you believed best fit you.

The same goes for your first job. There will be a dozen companies that you will want to work for and a couple that your parents may suggest. You will fill out applications, interview for positions, visit the office, and get as much information on the company as you can. While you won't get offered a position at every company where you apply, you will ultimately choose a job with one of the companies that makes an offer and that you believe will be a good fit for you.

You probably had one school in particular that for one reason or another just didn't work out. The same will happen in your job hunt. There will be job that looks perfect, but just not work out for some reason. Don't be discouraged. Keep up the hunt and another job will come along soon.

In the end, you might not take the highest paying job, just like you might not choose the school with the cheapest tuition. What it comes down to is picking a job that is the best fit for you and gives you the best chance to excel at what you wish to pursue.

▶ Life Before Noon Tip

Without putting much thought into it, write down five local companies and five national companies that you feel would be a good fit with you. Do you notice any similarities? Now, do some research on the Internet to find other companies which are similar in size and industry.

Attending Class Is Just Like Going To Work

College is filled with different classes to take. Think of class as your job. There is a start time and an end time. Will you ever be running late? Of course. Do it enough times, though, and your professor will let you hear about it and probably invite you to take the course again next semester.

Failing the semester is the equivalent of being fired from your job. Making the grade or doing your job well should be motivation enough; don't let something as petty as punctuality come back to bite you in the ass. The sooner you realize that what you do today is practice for tomorrow, the better.

You probably liked to cut it close most of the time and arrive to class right when it started. When you did arrive early there were benefits that came with it. You got the seat you wanted and were able to compare your homework with your classmates to make any last second changes. Plus, it gave you some social time with your classmates.

The same happens at work. While it might seem silly for you to show up at 8:45 a.m. when you don't officially start getting paid until 9 a.m., it is worth it in the long run. You have some time to socialize, get organized and get some last minute work done on something you may have forgotten about. Plus, your boss will love that you are always there early.

Once you are into your career it will be easier to identify things with past experiences. If you can develop the discipline now, it will put you one step ahead of your competition after college. Employers are going to want someone who is ready to work and able to step in with the smallest learning curve. You, of course, will have to learn about the job itself, but the preparedness you undergo in college will allow you to apply this knowledge in any job in any field. Realize this now, and it will pay off later.

▶ Life Before Noon Tip

Plan on getting to work 15 minutes early each day. That way if you are running a little late, you will at the very least end up on time.

Your Classmates Are Just Like Co-Workers

You had classmates in every class you took. Think of them as your co-workers. As you probably have realized since grade school, you did NOT get along with all of your classmates and the same goes for co-workers. The key is not to worry about getting along with them but rather knowing how to work with them.

You spent roughly four hours a week in class with your classmates, but you are going to be spending 40 hours a week at the office with your co-workers. All the group projects and class discussions were great practice for your career. Learning how to speak up in class in front of someone you may not like is going to come in handy when you find yourself in a meeting with people whom you do not necessarily agree with.

All of our lives we have practiced getting along with others, but in college it was one of the most important non-academic lessons you learned. The classroom forced you to open up and contribute to a conversation or project. By doing this it gave you a chance to hear what other people had to say as well as form an opinion on what kind of worker they were.

When it came time to form study groups or work on group projects, you wanted to team up with those students who spoke intelligently in class, because you knew they were current on the assignments and worked hard. The same speaks true at your job. You are going to want to know who has their shit together so you can bounce ideas off of them or team up with them on projects. Chances are that they're are not the ones who are constantly late or always leaving early.

▶ **Life Before Noon Tip**

Get in the practice of remembering people's names. Nothing is stranger than being with the same company for two years with the same guy and always just saying, "What's up dude?" Knowing people's names right away will accelerate your acceptance in the work environment.

◇ Lesson 24 ◇

Your Professor Is Just Like A Boss

Every class had a professor. Think of him (don't give us a hard time about being sexist, this is just the easiest way to convey our point) as a boss. We have never taken a class where there weren't mixed reviews on a professor. Some thought he was too nice, while others thought he was a prick. Some loved his teaching methods, while others felt he wasn't challenging enough. Some said he showed favoritism, while others complained he just overall wasn't fair. The same goes for bosses.

All of the things that your professor did or didn't do can be taken as a learning experience for working for your boss. When you accept a job you also accept a boss. Not all bosses are the best, but you must learn to work for them and with them.

Take the time to find out what your boss likes and dislikes. Complete projects in a format he likes. Prioritize things as your boss wants them, not on what you think is most important. These aren't going to be things you can figure out on the first day, but as you grow in your job (just as the semester moved on) you learn what works and what doesn't.

Remember, since your boss hired you, you represent him. No boss wants one of his hires to be a problem and have to fire them. It is embarrassing for them and reflects poorly on their decision making.

Same goes for you time in school. If you flunked a class, it showed poorly on your professor and his job educating you.

▶ **Life Before Noon Tip**

Don't talk about your boss behind his back. You never know which one of your co-workers knows him on a personal level.

Your Classroom Is Just Like An Office

Every class you signed up for was held in some type of classroom. Think of that classroom as your office. Some of us chose class solely on proximity to our living quarters. The same is true for work. Money may be tight at first and so geographical location is important. Gas prices may influence how far you want to travel to work each day.

The classroom was also a place that you went to get something accomplished. You should have the same attitude in the office. You can still have fun and crack jokes with your friends as long as you realize that you still have to get things done. If you are that guy who is never serious and doesn't come through when needed, then people will not want to work with you. You want to let people know that you can have a laid back attitude and that pressure doesn't get to you, but when it comes down to it you will get the job done.

Where you sat in the classroom often reflected what type of worker you were. If you sat up front then classmates perceived you as a brown-noser. If you sat in the back then you were too cool for class. Understand that you are an adult now and the "cool" kids don't sit in the back. The ones who sit in the back during meetings will be the ones in a couple of years asking "do you want fries with that?"

▶ **Life Before Noon Tip**

On your first day on the job, you don't have to accept the first place they give you. Start to move your desk and cabinet around so you feel comfortable. Also, try to position your computer screen so people can't tell if you are working or surfing the Internet.

◇ **Lesson 26** ◇

Your Homework Is Just Like Work Assignments

Every class you had assigned homework and projects. When you are working after college your day will be filled with similar duties. You will learn which of these you can half-ass and which you need to bust ass. All the work you did in the classroom will help develop the work ethic you need for your job.

Your boss will judge you on the body of work and the results you produce. You aren't going to receive a promotion after every task done well, but after each one you will be noticed a little bit more, and over time it will add up in your favor. Know that your work is a reflection of you.

The biggest thing you can take from having to do assignments in college is time management and justifying your work. Odds are that you will not have to do any word problems or essays in your job, but you will need to get things done on time and have facts to support your decisions. College is a very opinionated environment where there isn't always one answer to a question. The same goes for your career. Lots of questions will be presented to you, and it is your responsibility to produce the best recommendation.

When your boss asks you for some analysis or a report, be sure to ask when he wants it. If he has you working on multiple projects and assigns a new one, be sure to ask him which one he wants done first. Sometimes your boss needs something for his own needs and other times his boss is asking for something.

When working on your assignments, check with your boss once you have a working copy to make sure you are heading in the right direction. Things change fast in the business world, and he might want you to change the assignment to something else which has become more important.

▶ **Life Before Noon Tip**

Format your reports and charts in the same format as your boss does. Use the same font, size, spacing, and page orientation. Name the file in the same format that you boss uses. This will be a blessing to your boss because everything is in the format that he likes, and he won't have to adjust the file after he receives it from you.

Spring Break Is
Just Like A Work Vacation

Spring break was a time for fun without worries. It was always easier to plan ahead and get work done so you didn't have anything to worry about when you return. Work is the same way. You will want to have everything prepared so that there are no hiccups in your absence and nothing urgent due upon return that could have been done before you left. Vacations are important to everyone and short ones need to be taken a couple of times a year.

In college, spring breaks were centered around parties and boozing. Beaches and nightlife were the main hotspots. Once you are in your career this may change, but it doesn't have to. Vacations should be a release and a time to cut loose with friends.

The big difference between the two is that in college you had a day or two to catch up on sleep before classes resume mid-week. Once you are in your career, you will need to be on your A-game first thing Monday morning. Be sure to factor recovery time into your vacation and don't rely on easing back into a schedule during the work week.

Vacations spent partying may not be an option financially when beginning your career. There is nothing wrong with making it a cheap vacation but still having a lot of fun. Just staying home and sleeping in will become a great vacation option (We know how lame that sounds right now, but it is the truth.)

Most other young professionals will be in the same boat so don't think you always have to go all-out on your vacation. Whether you decide to take vacation out of town or stay in town, enjoy it like you did in college and be sure to take care of responsibilities at work just like you did in the classroom.

▶ Life Before Noon Tip

> *In the work world, it is better to spread out your vacations into a bunch of three-day and four-day weekends then just taking all your vacation at once. Not only will you be able to do a lot of different things, but you also will not be letting work pile up while you are gone for weeks at a time.*

◇ Lesson 28 ◇

Throwing A Keg Party Is Just Like Event Planning

Many corporate jobs involve events. Anyone who has planned a party, chaired on a social committee, or been involved with any Greek affiliation has experience in this field.

In college you may have had a budget of $300 at the most which included kegs, pizza, and possibly some illegal substances. In the corporate world, your budget will be hundreds of thousands of dollars. Don't let this intimidate you. Instead, know that you have been doing this all through school, and now you have an opportunity to expand your knowledge and take an event to the next level.

There is certainly going to be a corporate standard that you will need to follow in order to keep your job and work with corporate clients. Whatever it is that you decide to do, don't conform too much. The reason someone hired you is because you had something that others didn't. If parties you threw in college were successful, then have the confidence that your work events will follow the same pattern.

It is also important to be social with those around you. People want to be around someone who is fun and still gets their work done. All the time you spent in college hanging out with groups of people and partying will actually pay off in the long run. It taught you how to meet new people, and more importantly, make them feel welcome. This is one of those lessons learned outside of the classroom. Just by having fun you will be so far ahead of the bookworm who got straight A's, who didn't know how to interact with people in college, and won't know how to interact with co-workers.

▶ Life Before Noon Tip

Don't focus too much on the glamorous details of the event. Make sure you have the basics of food, drink, staff, and entertainment before you start to even think about an ice sculpture (although ice blocks were a tremendous touch at any college party).

Lessons Learned ◇ 33 ◇

Selling T-Shirts Is
Just Like Entrepreneurship

One thing that is constant throughout the years is that money is rare in school. People will take on just about any part-time job available including cleaning kennels at an animal hospital for minimum wage (we know this one from experience.) Every time you work a crappy job just to make ends meet and think to yourself how you should just start your own business, you are on your way to being an entrepreneur.

Take the student who prints their own hilarious expressions on T-shirts and then hawks them at football games. This student is investing his own time and money for a profit. No one is hiring him to do this. He came up with an idea, planned it out, and executed without any "boss" telling him to do it.

Another example of an entrepreneur in school is a tutor. Tutors are not in it to help you. They are in it to make money. They have knowledge for which someone else is willing to pay. The more they tutor, the more money they make.

Besides making money, being an entrepreneur while in school helped develop skills that will pay dividends down the road. First, if you don't get a job when you graduate, you could keep a steady income by continuing your business. Second, entrepreneurial skills are valuable in companies. Not only do small, nimble organizations love entrepreneurs, but big corporations love people with entrepreneurial skills to jump-start ideas among co-workers. Finally, the small idea you started in college to earn a few bucks can turn into a big deal down the road. Microsoft, Google, and Facebook were all small businesses started by students in college.

You might think that starting your own business is tough. It is not. Think about parties you threw in college. You bought a keg for $50, collected $5 from 20 people and just like that your money was doubled. It's that easy. Build a strong foundation for your business and then start to think big.

▶ **Life Before Noon Tip**

> *Don't just let your college entrepreneurial ideas just die when you graduate and leave the college town. Hire a young student to run the business for you. It might just turn into something big in a few years.*

◇ Lesson 30 ◇

Going Out To Bars Is Just Like Networking

Although networking is not a career, it is certainly something that you will use frequently. Networking events are organized everyday for different industries. Most large employers will put all new hires in a training session that will likely be spread out over several days. Sure there is going to be a lot of useful information gained, but just as important will be how you interact with new people.

It is an opportunity to meet colleagues in similar fields and also an opportunity get your name out there and possibly better your future. Going to bars or parties to meet up with your friends and meet new people is the same exact thing. Sure the agendas will be different, but the principal is the same. You are going into a social situation with the expectation of finding something.

In college, your goal may be to get laid. After graduation, your goal may be to land a job. The desired outcome is different, but the manner in getting there is the same. Several of our friends were offered jobs in college after we ran into executives at our local bars who simply liked how we handled ourselves in social situations.

Don't be intimidated by someone because they may have 30 years under their belt. If that guy or girl in the bar thought you were intimidated then you probably wouldn't have gotten laid. Don't let fear of the unknown prohibit you in any way. In 30 years you will know much more than any executive today.

▶ Life Before Noon Tip

Continue to frequent your favorite bar but always make occasional appearances at different bars. By changing it up so you have a chance to meet new people and interact in a different environment. The way you act in a martini bar is much different than a sports bar. You need to be able to adapt on the fly, and that only comes from experience.

◇ 4 ◇

FINDING A JOB
MARKET YOURSELF BETTER THAN
YOUR COMPETITION

Prime yourself for a job. You will need to sell yourself to potential employers. Most students don't know how to interview so they go into the process timid and shy. Eliminate your competition by knowing everything about the interview process before it starts. Plus, avoid stupid mistakes that people make every day simply because they don't know better (and haven't read this book)!

- ✓ Lesson 31: Get Involved In The Career Services Center
- ✓ Lesson 32: Schedule As Many Interviews As Possible
- ✓ Lesson 33: Don't Let Starting Salaries Concern You
- ✓ Lesson 34: Be Presentable And Leave A Lasting Impression
- ✓ Lesson 35: Job Fairs Are Not For Losers
- ✓ Lesson 36: Check On Alumni Perks
- ✓ Lesson 37: Find Your Local Alumni Chapter
- ✓ Lesson 38: First Comes Work, Then Comes Play
- ✓ Lesson 39: Can't We All Just Get Along
- ✓ Lesson 40: How To Keep Yourself Employed During Tough Times

◇ Lesson 31 ◇
Get Involved In The Career Services Center

We know you probably had better things to do (drinking, sleeping, sleeping with someone after drinking...) than spend time in the Career Services Center, but this is a mandatory for all soon-to-be or recently graduated. Your school Career Services Center connects companies looking to hire with students who want jobs. Don't think that it is a waste of time to participate in this FREE service. It is the job of the employees in the career services center to get their students a job. Also, companies don't waste time and money. If they are sending staff down to fill open positions with students, you know they are serious about hiring.

The first step is to schedule an appointment with the Career Services Center. They will help you develop a resume that will be presentable to upcoming interviewers. Ideally you will want to do this your junior year to get a head start because some companies only conduct interviews once a semester. If college is quickly dwindling down, DON'T FREAK OUT. Career Services will also have access to an alumni database that can keep you in the job opening loop even after graduation, but the sooner you begin the better.

Many students will never take advantage of this and they will be the ones who are stuck in their college town working as a bar back at age 35. In the words of Jeremy Piven in *PCU*, "Don't be that guy." The Career Services Center will also provide mock interview sessions that will help prepare you for the real interview.

You will be able to view a list of companies that are scheduling interviews. When there is an interview posting, try to get the last slot of the day. While common sense would be that the interviewer would be tired and not paying attention at this point, the truth is that you will be in the interviewer's mind more than those who interviewed earlier. Most interviewers get lost and start forgetting who's who after eight interviews.

▶ Life Before Noon Tip

Make sure to have all of your necessary information ready before going to Career Services for resume help (ex: addresses, dates of employment, reference information, etc.)

Schedule As Many Interviews As Possible

If you are a marketing major, don't just interview for jobs that are in sales or advertising. If you are a finance major, don't just interview with accounting firms. Interview for restaurants, banks, sales, retail, and whatever else seems even remotely interesting. Your field of study can be applied to any career.

Every interview is an opportunity for practice. You will find that there are common questions in every interview. For example, every interviewer will ask you some form of "Why do you want to work for us?" You can easily prepare a universal answer that may have to only be tweaked slightly for each interviewer.

After your first couple of interviews you will learn which questions are consistent. Take the time to prepare generic answers to these questions so you will go into the interview relaxed because you know what questions are coming. On the same note, make your first couple of interviews with companies you are not very interested in. This will allow you to get all of the mistakes and nervousness out of the way.

Another advantage to interviewing as much as possible is that you may find something that is a good fit that wasn't even on your radar. Don't be choosy when it comes to job opportunities. It is similar to applying for colleges. You want to have a couple of job opportunities locked up before graduation. It is AMAZING how much pressure will come off once you have a job lined up. You can spend the rest of your college days breezing through classes and living up your last days in school while everyone panics trying to find a job.

▶ **Life Before Noon Tip**

Show up at least 15 minutes early for your interview so you can calmly review any notes. Also, don't forget breath mints!

Don't Let Starting Salaries Concern You

All of us plan on making the big bucks someday. None of us should plan on making it right out of college. There is a correlation between money and experience. Since you have little experience coming out of college, you shouldn't expect much money. You have to start at the bottom and work your way up.

Realize that your starting salary is exactly that. It is a start. Do what you can to get ahead and the money will follow. Take a job for the opportunity, not the salary. There are very few, if any, jobs that will have high starting salaries. Take a job where you can excel and make more money in the long run.

Why are starting salaries so low? Because they can be. Jobs pay what they do because of the demand for the job. Entry level salary positions are sought after by not only recent college graduates but also by the hourly employees at the company. With so many people trying to get the same job, there is no incentive to pay more money. Companies will pay the least amount they have to.

Higher level salary positions require certain expertise that many people do not have, so it is actually difficult to find candidates for the positions. Usually companies have to look to steal employees at other companies by offering them a higher salary.

Once you are in a company, bounce around in different positions and gain all the experience you can while you don't have as many personal responsibilities. One day you may have a family, and it won't be as easy to move around and change pace so quickly.

▶ Life Before Noon Tip

Starting salaries are just that...starting salaries. At least if it is really low, you have no where to go but up.

Be Presentable And Leave A Lasting Impression

Always remember that you can only make a first impression once. Whether you think it is right or wrong, you will be judged on appearance. Make sure that you are presentable at all times, especially in the beginning.

Appearance is also a state of mind. It is hard to concentrate if you are underdressed. You will constantly be worrying about what people think and how embarrassed you are that you did not take the time to properly prepare. Employers will view this as irresponsible and unprepared.

Imagine that you went on a first date and your counterpart showed up looking like he or she had just woken up. You would think that they weren't that into you, and you would be turned off. Your boss would feel the same way if you were not presentable. This also can go the way of overdressing. Feel confident in what you wear and keep it unique if you like, but be sure that it still falls in the presentable guidelines.

After an interview, be sure to keep in touch with the interviewer. Follow up the interview with a simple email letting the interviewer know that you appreciated the time and are interested in a career with them. The interviewer probably had many interviews that day so any opportunity to standout (in a good way) will benefit you in the long run.

If you wait too long to make contact with the employer then they may not even remember you, and it could lead to some unwanted awkwardness. It is the same awkwardness that you feel when you haven't talked to your parents in weeks and don't have any excuse why you haven't.

▶ Life Before Noon Tip

During this process you probably will not interview with the same person more than once. Buy a simple suit and a couple of shirts and ties. That is all. You don't need a different suit for each interview.

Job Fairs Are Not For Losers

Job fairs come across as a "cattle call." You probably think you are better than that. Really, stand in line to be interviewed? Yes, because job fairs offer the opportunity to view many different companies that are actually going to hire. Since the company paid money to participate, their recruiters will look like they didn't do their job if they come back empty handed. In other words, each company at the job fair will be making job offers.

Job fairs are a great way to get interview "screens" with many different companies in one day. Most college job fairs will have more than 50 companies in attendance. These companies will set up booths and have plenty of information available. Don't think that you will have an official interview opportunity. You will, however, have an opportunity to get your name and resume out there.

Be presentable when you show up. So many students act like these job fairs are no big deal. They stop by in shorts and sandals on their way to run errands thinking they can drop a couple of resumes off. This is yet another opportunity for you to separate yourself from others simply by being presentable. Companies will take note of this, and it will help you out. Remember that even though it is not an official interview it is still your first impression. Make it a good one and make it count.

Saturate the job fair and pass out as many resumes as you can. However, don't go down each row and just pass it out to everyone. Companies may not take you seriously and simply toss it in the garbage because they figure that you don't really care about their specific company. Spread things out and visit booths randomly. This way you can visit all the booths without looking like you are in an assembly line. Also, be sure to make it a priority to see the booths you are most interested in first. At some point there will probably be a line and you don't want to run out of time.

Companies usually hire entry level hourly people at job fairs. You won't get a high paying manager position, but possibly a supervisor position that has great potential for growth.

► **Life Before Noon Tip**

> *Research the list of upcoming job fair attendees and learn a couple of things about your top three choices so you have something to talk about at the event.*

◇ Lesson 36 ◇

Check On Alumni Perks

A hiring manager will always give someone from his or her alma mater the edge over another equally qualified candidate. The reason behind this is shared experience. If managers can find some commonality between them and a potential hire, then it will give them some peace of mind. They feel it will be easier to build a relationship. Be sure to check potential employers that have ties to your school, because it may make a very easy and successful job lead.

Colleges keep in touch with their alumni because of the amount of money that alumni provide. Colleges are not financially dependent strictly on alumni, but they do rely heavily on their support. With that being said, colleges are very willing to offer things back to their alumni in exchange for their donations. Most schools will have an alumni donation package that is very doable for the newly graduated.

Alumni perks may include deals on season tickets, hard-to-get away game tickets, and most importantly, ongoing access to job openings through the Career Services Center or networking opportunities. Take the time before graduation to stop by your alumni center and get all the information. As graduation nears there will be plenty to keep you busy, and you don't want this to go by the wayside.

▶ Life Before Noon Tip

Many times an alumni foundation can have connections to different jobs. Speak with them about what alumni job connections may be available in your desired geographic location.

◊ Lesson 37 ◊
Find Your Local Alumni Chapter

If you have your job lined up or you know what city is the next stop for you, go ahead and take the time to find your local alumni chapter. The chapter can help you land a job or make the moving transition easier by introducing you to some people in the area who share similar interests. Either way this is yet another networking opportunity for you and allows you to continue your success.

More importantly, this is another opportunity to gain an advantage with little to no financial obligation. Most local alumni chapters have yearly dues of $10 to $20 which gives you access to all social events. Local chapters also organize great game watching events for those fans who can't travel to the games.

If you are fortunate enough to have your first job be the same one you retire from some 40 years later, then consider yourself lucky and double down at your local casino! For us other mere mortals it is very common to jump around a little bit before you find your dream job (or at least one you can tolerate for an extended period of time). It is much easier to pursue job leads through a networking group like your local alumni chapter than it is to search random ones online. Not only will you have an easier path to getting hired, but you also share common interests with people in the group so the job will probably be something right up your alley.

▶ **Life Before Noon Tip**

Local alumni chapters can be a great source for job leads or networking. They are also a great way to meet women with the same interests. Think of it as a 2-for-1 special.

◇ **Lesson 38** ◇

First Comes Work, Then Comes Play

Once you do find the career that suits you best, time management is something that you must master and practice everyday. If you wake up to an alarm, you are practicing time management. If you scheduled no classes on Fridays because your favorite bar had a happy hour on Thursday that started at 9 p.m. and you knew you would be too hung over to go to class, you practiced time management.

Just like your teacher, your boss will expect you to be on time. If they expect you to be on time then exceed expectations and show up early. Something as simple as punctuality could be what separates you from slacker co-workers.

Use the time before you begin your career to begin developing good habits. Whether your first class is at noon or you have a few weeks before work starts, start to wake up at 7 a.m. Use a couple of weeks or months to hit the snooze button and miss your alarm. You would rather do it now when it doesn't affect anything then as a new employee trying to prove yourself.

When you start your career, you will be tempted to go out all the time. You will finally have money and other people will always be going out for a drink after work. You need to have an excuse in your back pocket at all times (a hot date is always an acceptable one), so you don't get pulled in to hanging out at the local Applebee's bar until 1 a.m.

▶ **Life Before Noon Tip**

In college, practice time management in a practical way. Use football season to set your alarm early so you get up in time to tailgate. It is the same concept, just a different goal.

Can't We All Just Get Along

Once you begin work, your attitude and compatibility with others will be just as important as your abilities. Many sports professionals bounce around from team to team because they simply cannot get along with others, and it causes uneasiness in the locker room. Just like sports organizations, businesses are successful if they run as one, cohesive unit. Having the approval and cooperation of your co-workers will allow you to not only perform well, but also move up in the company.

Employers are going to look for someone who can not only get the job done but also work well with others and get the best out of them. If you missed a class and needed to get notes from someone it wouldn't be possible if you hadn't previously interacted with them or if they don't like you. Just like you depended on classmates in college you will depend on co-workers in your job.

Managers may not be the most experienced in their field or even the best at everything their job encompasses. They are in management because they can get people to work together and excel at their respective positions. While you are in an entry level position, be sure to use that time to sharpen your people skills and learn how to work with others. People at different levels tend to use "different" languages so be sure to also learn how to communicate on different levels of the hierarchy.

Always be social with your co-workers. Some of them will be older than your parents and may feel threatened by a young man like yourself. Talk to them about sports, politics, current events, or anything that you may have in common. They need to know that you are approachable for them to value you.

◣ **Life Before Noon Tip**

> *Make yourself available for office social events, especially at the beginning, even if you'd rather not go. It is important to get to know your co-workers in a social atmosphere, because building a relationship will help out everyone in the office.*

How To Keep Yourself Employed During Tough Times

Securing a job is a large part of the battle, but unfortunately it is not the only part. Economies and businesses are inevitably going to go through hard times, and layoffs or cutbacks are going to happen. When executives look to layoff people they go after the ones whose departure will have the least impact on current business. Make yourself a vital part of the business so you are not even on their layoff radar.

The first step is to involve yourself in daily company tasks. If there is a new report that goes out each morning to the executives, volunteer to be the one that puts it together and sends it out. Do simple activities such as brewing the coffee, fixing the copier, putting up the big water bottles, and getting the mail. While these don't seem like any big deal, people will think you are always there taking care of things.

Another step is to appear more dedicated than your co-workers. Start work before they do, work through lunch, stay late, and stop by on weekends for a couple of hours. While they have to leave at 6 p.m. to go pick up their kids, you have the flexibility to work all hours of the day and night. In layoff times, you have to show dedication.

Finally, don't give up your secrets on accomplishments. You don't want to lie to anyone, but instead of just passing knowledge out so someone else can complete the task, make yourself available and show that you need to be there for things to get done. Also, if a task is really easy for you to do but everyone else thinks it is "rocket science," there is nothing wrong with keeping them in the dark.

If you are doing the job you are capable of, you won't have to worry about losing it. However, if there are tough times and cuts need to be made, it will be harder to cut someone who is always available and always contributing.

▶ Life Before Noon Tip

Make it a point to involve yourself with projects outside of your department. If there is a Safety Team or an Evacuation Team, be the first to volunteer. Getting involved with corporate projects is a great way to be noticed.

◇ 5 ◇

FUNCTIONING IN THE WORKPLACE
EASY WAYS TO JOB ADVANCEMENT

How to use the skills you know already to make headway in the office environment. Don't be complacent in your job just because you are excited to have one. Take the social skills you developed in college and apply them to your career. Learn easy ways to get in good with the boss and what you need to do every day that will put your career path on the fast track.

- ✓ Lesson 41: Know Your Boss
- ✓ Lesson 42: Develop A Good Persona With Co-Workers
- ✓ Lesson 43: How To Make "More for Nothing" Count
- ✓ Lesson 44: Cross-Train
- ✓ Lesson 45: Dealing With Time And Waiting For Opportunity
- ✓ Lesson 46: Keys To Getting A Raise
- ✓ Lesson 47: Inter-Department Etiquette
- ✓ Lesson 48: Moonlighting
- ✓ Lesson 49: You Are Your Job
- ✓ Lesson 50: Take Some Internet Or Distance Learning Classes

◇ Lesson 41 ◇

Know Your Boss

Most direct bosses will be personable and down to Earth. Let's face it, if they weren't then you probably wouldn't be as excited to be working there. Your boss is going to expect the same of you. Become knowledgeable in some of the things that your boss enjoys.

If it is something you are completely not interested in, then don't feel like you have to sell out to get on his good side. If it is something you are mildly interested in, then try paying a little more attention so you can contribute to the next conversation. For example, if you already like sports but you are not much of a hockey fan and your boss is, go ahead and pay a little more attention. If he is a strong Democrat and you are a diehard Republican, don't think that you need to change your views to agree with his. Just avoid the political conversations.

There is going to be a correlation between your work ethic and your boss's attitude toward you. Your boss will be more likely to give you those extra days off if he knows that you are willing to work late when needed or come in on the occasional off day. Also, once you have your duties pretty much under control don't be afraid to ask for more work. Your boss will like the initiative and will go to you for future projects. Once you accept a job and a salary, it is rare that anyone is going to pay you more money without a reason. If you want more money then you will either have to get promoted or take on more work in your current job.

You don't have to do your co-worker's job so they can take it easy, just let your boss know you are looking to learn more and take on new tasks. If you don't think something is absolutely necessary to bring to your boss's attention, then don't. Anything you can take care of on your own, will help give him more time to do his job. If you feel confident you can handle something on your own then go ahead and do it. Once you are done, you can review how you came to your decision with your boss and then go from there.

▶ Life Before Noon Tip

> *Your boss is your life line. He brought you in to the company, and he can take you out. Stay on his good side, no matter what.*

◇ Lesson 42 ◇
Develop A Good Persona With Co-Workers

From the day you start work, you will see which co-workers "get it." They understand the company culture, are positive about their work, have a good relationship with their boss, and have respect from co-workers.

Model yourself after these people. Don't go up to them and ask to be their "protégé," but do ask them for advice and bounce ideas off of them. They want to teach you and show you the ropes. They will respect that you want to learn and that you are not a stuck up kid who thinks he knows everything in the world.

The next step is learning how to deal with co-workers in a team environment. Throughout school you have been doing group work and been participating in study groups. Remember, your classmates are just like co-workers. Instead of studying together, you work together. You will have to learn their strengths and weaknesses, because your success as a team will depend on everyone. If someone is not very personable then they may be better suited for a job where they don't have direct contact with people. Just like in class if someone is not a very good speaker then you wouldn't want them to give the presentation or at least you would have them speak as little as possible.

It is also good to spend time with co-workers out of work to let them know that you are just like them. No one likes a co-worker who doesn't like to hang out outside of work and who always eats lunch with the boss. That leads to the label of a brown-noser. You want to make sure that you have a good relationship with co-workers because the cohesiveness of the group will be critical to your success.

▶ **Life Before Noon Tip**

> *When you are out for drinks with co-workers, don't just drink off of them. Offer to buy a round or two. Most young people think that the person who makes the most money should be buying. If you mooch off of them, they won't respect you, and they won't view you as an equal.*

How To Make
"More For Nothing" Count

One of the biggest mistakes you can make as a young professional is NOT doing something because there is no extra pay. If your boss comes to you and asks you to step up to the plate in someone's absence, without any change to your salary, be sure to accept the challenge. Accomplishing the project may be a necessary step to the next promotion.

First off, your boss will appreciate you "going the extra mile" and taking on additional duties. Secondly, it will be something for you to bring up at your next review or in an interview. Everyone likes someone who is willing to take on more work. Plus, your boss would not ask to you take on additional work if you were not already doing a good job. Finally, if you are going out of your way to take on more responsibility without pay then they will not get as mad at you if something goes wrong. If your boss knows you are going above and beyond, then they will be more lenient with minor mistakes because they know your plate is fully loaded.

Taking on extra work and doing a good job with it will ultimately lead to more money. Even though it may not be immediate, show some patience and know in the end that the reward will be there. Don't be afraid to make a suggestion. Too many times people don't speak up and end up missing out on great recognition that could put them above their co-workers and help take them to the next level.

As you take on more and more, some of the older co-workers may try to knock you back down so it doesn't look like they are slacking. Don't be intimidated by them. Keep up the hard work.

▶ **Life Before Noon Tip**

Don't brag to your co-workers about how hard and long you work. They don't care, and it will only make you look like you are doing it because you are trying to get recognition. Just keep cranking along, getting as much done as fast and accurately as possible. Let your work speak for itself.

◇ Lesson 44 ◇

Cross-Train

One of the most valuable tools you can have is to be knowledgeable in more than one field. Do a great job in your job, but also become familiar with different jobs or departments. If you and another employee each make $30,000, but an employer realizes that he can pay you $50,000 to do both jobs, then he will make the choice that saves him $10,000. Plus you end up with a 66 percent salary increase.

The best employees are those who can answer questions about all aspects of the company. You don't need to know everything about every position, but you want to know enough about all of them. Don't be afraid to bounce around between different departments and shadow them to get a better understanding. The president of the company will not know all the details about each department, but they will know very well how each one operates so they can make sound business decisions. If it worked for them, why won't it work for you?

Learn as much as possible about your company to become a better employee right away. You will understand why other departments do things the way they do and that will help you in your daily operation. The other obvious advantage to cross-training is that you may find another job within the company that you like better. Don't limit yourself to the position you started at within the company or the path that particular job may take you. Keep your options open and your stock high.

▶ Life Before Noon Tip

Talk to other co-workers about how their departments work. You don't want to work in a departmental silo and not fully understand how everything is interconnected.

◇ **Lesson 45** ◇

Dealing With Time And Waiting For Opportunity

Wanting to take the world by storm and getting promoted in three months is a great goal, but it usually doesn't happen that fast. It may not even happen in the first year. Hard work is not the only thing needed to get a promotion. There needs to be an opportunity.

You might get frustrated, working so hard and not seeing any immediate benefit. You will find people that make just as much money as you, but they work half as hard. Don't fall into that group. Ten years from now they will still be doing the same thing while you will be wildly successful.

Stay focused and keep up the hard work. Opportunity arises quickly, and you need to be there to grab it.

Once you get your first opportunity for a promotion, it puts you on the radar and opens up more windows for you. Don't settle once you've found yourself a solid job. Keep pushing for more. Other companies like to steal the rising stars of their competitors, so if you land a promotion early, be open to talking with other companies. Wanting to spend your entire career with one company and showing them loyalty is a fine attribute; just make sure they pay you what you are worth.

▶ **Life Before Noon Tip**

You may have to take a lateral move in order to get a promotion. Don't get frustrated if you are switching departments and taking on more responsibilities but still getting paid the same. If you keep up the dedication, your time will come.

Keys To Getting A Raise

Great productivity and how you work with others will be the reasons you get a raise. No one is going to give a raise simply because they like you. With that being said, it is easier to get a raise if you have a good social relationship with your boss.

Be sure to include yourself in different activities. If your boss asks you to complete a project that you have no interest in be sure not to turn him down! He may be testing you to see how open you are to new ideas (we repeat some concepts to stress their importance.) Be sure to take charge in any project, but be careful how you approach it. Working well with others is pertinent to any promotion. You can do the best work in the company, but if people don't like you or don't want to work with you, then you will not get promoted.

Take every opportunity to be the lead on any project. This means taking on more work, even if it does not immediately result in a pay increase. Your boss will want to see how you perform in a management position before he pays you for it. In sports it is unlikely that a team is going to invest big bucks in a player before they see him/her perform. This is the same concept.

You are going to have to pay your dues just like when you were a freshman. Don't let anything deter you. Take advantage of every opportunity, and make it a point to include everyone when there is a group project. Find out how to exploit strengths and hide weaknesses. How well you combine all these factors will determine how far you move up in the company.

▶ **Life Before Noon Tip**

When paying your dues in your career just be happy that it is easier than when you were a fraternity pledge paying your dues. Anything you have to do at work is better than the paddles and blindfolds that you faced during Hell Week.

Inter-Department Etiquette

Trust is a very important quality between boss and employee. Your boss has to trust that you will not only get the project completed on time but that it will also be done well. Your boss will also trust you with information that should not be shared with the public, your co-workers, or both.

Inter-department meetings are sometimes an opportunity for departments to "vent" with other departments. One of the quickest ways to get on your boss' bad side is to mention your own frustrations to other departments. It is fine to have friends outside of your department, but airing dirty laundry is a no-no. Keep inter-department discussions where they there are supposed to be: within the department. The last thing they want you to do is start some rumor that will result in a tough and awkward working environment.

Another trust factor regards the information that you will be privileged with knowing. Sometimes it is thought to be common sense that certain numbers should not be discussed outside of the office, but if you have any questions about it, be sure to ask. There is probably a privacy clause that you will need to sign prior to employment that states any violation is subject to termination. When in doubt, just keep it to yourself!

▶ **Life Before Noon Tip**

Live by this rule: what happens in your department stays in your department.

◇ Lesson 48 ◇
Moonlighting

Moonlighting simply means working a "side" job in addition to your regular job. Your side job will probably not match the income of your regular job nor can it suffice as your sole income. Rather, it is a job to make some extra money or pursue something that you may one day want to make a career.

Being fresh out of college, you won't have as many priorities at home, like a family, so you can afford to pick up extra jobs here and there for more money. It may be a job where you work from your house or help out on projects in the evenings or weekends. Don't miss an opportunity to make money and learn a skill set that may not be available in your current job.

If you don't need the extra money, but are interested in doing more, then go ahead and be picky about your side job. Become self-employed in a field that really interests you. Doing something like writing a book or blog may seem pretty simple, but there is much more that goes into it. The writing process is an obvious learning experience, but you also can work on marketing your product, how to work with agents and being your own public relations department. If you are going to do something on the side then be sure that you will enjoy it. It will be cutting into your downtime.

If you are trying to decide whether or not to take on an additional job then ask yourself, "What is more valuable? One hour of work, or one hour on your project?" If you are working six days a week and work 12 hours a day, then you know you don't have time to pick up a side job for entertainment. However, if spending a little bit of time on a project of your own that will not only produce a little income but will also help you develop skills necessary for advancement in any job, then why not take a shot?

When you do take on a side job, be sure that there is no conflict of interest with your current employer. When in doubt, ask your boss.

▶ **Life Before Noon Tip**

> *Start a simple daily blog about something in which you have interest. While it might not be anything now, a couple years from now when you have thousands of entries, people will consider you an expert.*

You Are Your Job

Wherever it is you decide to work, be proud of it. You represent your company any time you are in the community or at any social gathering. If you get drunk and stupid at the bar and offend someone who knows where you work, not only will it look bad for you, but it will also look bad on the company. A company cannot afford to have someone employed who is going to bring bad press to the business. Whether you like it or not, there is a direct correlation between you and your company.

Keeping that in mind, live up to your job. If you are in sales and going to be traveling around to meet different clients, make sure your car is presentable. You don't have to drive a Ferrari, but you do want your car to be well kept. In this line of work, your first impression is often how you arrive. No one wants to do business with someone driving up in a beater with a crack in the windshield and one headlight out.

We know it isn't always easy to keep up with the maintenance on a car, so make sure you budget wisely. It is worth sacrificing something in order to keep your ride in top condition because it is an investment in yourself. It may only affect one lead/sale/offer, but that one sale is probably enough to offset any money you have put into your car and probably enough left over for a good, old-fashioned weekend bender.

As long as we are on the topic of representing your job, also realize that how you look will have an effect on your job performance. If someone has not taken care of their body or does not dress properly, then no one will take them seriously. Any client or co-worker will be thinking, "How can he help solve my problem if he can't even help himself?"

Take care of yourself and be presentable. Smelly shorts, backwards hats, and shirts with the front "frat tuck" will not work anymore. Realize that you are officially grown up and even though dressing professionally may not be your first choice, you will still have to dress the part to be successful. You can still show your individuality in your attire, just make sure it still fits in the appropriate guidelines.

▸ **Life Before Noon Tip**

Keep your clothes simple. Don't try to outdo others by buying expensive clothes and showing them off.

Take Some Internet Or Distance Learning Classes

Just because your first job is not your dream job does not make it the wrong job. Any opportunity you have to gain some work experience is a good one. If you know you do not want to be in a particular field for too much longer, then be sure to learn what you can while you are there. Gain simple, but valuable, job experience like waking up on time, dealing with co-workers, the cheapest way to pack a lunch, and whatever else you can. Do not just sit back and sulk until something else comes along. If you are going to wake up every day and go to work, you might as well accomplish something.

Another opportunity may be to take some online classes to help your resume. If you absolutely hate your job and are going to look for another one then you probably will have some extra time on your hands because you won't be the first guy to arrive and the last guy to leave. Use the extra time to your advantage. There are plenty of online courses available to help increase your knowledge.

The safest bet is to go with any business-related course. Business courses, such as marketing, can branch out into any job you will ever have. They touch on topics that everyone deals with on a regular basis like networking, advertising, and product placement. You may not be selling a physical product and only selling a service (doctor, accountant, lawyer...), but these courses can help you gain a competitive advantage in the marketplace. They show you how to make your service appear better than anyone else's. Perception is reality.

▶ **Life Before Noon Tip**

If you take supplemental classes after graduation be sure that the school is accredited so the classes will be viewed as acceptable by employers.

◇ **6** ◇

FINANCES
WHY A 24K GOLD TOOTHBRUSH
ISN'T NECESSARY

Don't succumb to the material things like 150-inch plasmas and Bentleys made out of diamonds. Set yourself up now with the right budget and get the most for your money. The toys will come later so it is not worth putting yourself in debt now (trust us, we know.)

- ✓ Lesson 51: Low Starting Salaries
- ✓ Lesson 52: Save Money By Eating Cheaply
- ✓ Lesson 53: Credit Cards Are Your New Best Friend (And Worst Enemy)
- ✓ Lesson 54: Give Back To Your School
- ✓ Lesson 55: Invest In Yourself
- ✓ Lesson 56: Graduate From College...And The Roller Skate Car
- ✓ Lesson 57: You Don't Need A 50-Inch Plasma, Even If You Can Afford It
- ✓ Lesson 58: We Know It Sounds Weak But Balance Your Checkbook
- ✓ Lesson 59: Write Your Personal Budget Down
- ✓ Lesson 60: Start Saving A Tiny Bit But Don't Tell Anyone

◇ Lesson 51 ◇

Low Starting Salaries

College has a funny way of really kicking you in the nuts sometimes. You take responsibility and attend class regularly (or as regularly as needed). You do well in class and make good grades (or good enough to pass; remember that Cs get degrees). You get some good interviews and accept a job. However, starting salaries don't afford you the ability to pay for that theatre room you planned on or that five-bedroom house.

Let's face it, even if you have a car you will be hard-pressed to fill it up with gas each week. So make sure that you take the time to lay out a budget before choosing housing or starting a job. This will help you account for all of your expenses and keep yourself out of a hole.

What is the real difference between $25,000 and $30,000 a year? After taxes, it totals roughly $67 a week. When you land the lower level jobs (you have to start somewhere), look for the other benefits. Does the office bring in bagels once a week? That is $6 in free food. Do they have a gourmet coffee maker so you don't have to hit up Starbucks? That is another $20 a week there.

Just like you had to monitor how many cafeteria meals per day or flex bucks you used, you will have to monitor expenses after college. Remember to live within your means. Tight budgets often lead to credit card trouble, something that should be avoided. Set a budget and then live within it.

▶ **Life Before Noon Tip**

Look for little ways to save money. Things like packing a lunch or having happy hour at home will allow you to save more money to purchase things you really need.

Save Money By Eating Cheaply

When you lived on campus you probably had a student account loaded up with money or food credits. You swiped your ID card once a day at the student cafeteria for your only meal of the day. That was not a typo in the previous sentence. In college you most likely lived off of one meal a day. If you woke up early enough for a quick breakfast snack then great, but most likely you slept in as long as possible and got up just in time for your first class.

After college, money will be even tighter, because all your bills will be paid by you. Try to be as frugal as those one-meal-a-day times. When you do decide to buy groceries, be sure to buy only necessary items. You don't need to load up on expensive alcohol or premium steaks. Remember what was available in the cafeteria and continue that trend. Mac and cheese, deli sandwiches, and burgers will get the job done. If you are having someone over for dinner then feel free to splurge, but for meals by yourself it isn't necessary.

Do you really need to eat something different each night? Do you really care about what you eat when you are eating by yourself? Go cheap and don't spend too much time creating some special, fancy dish. Just don't brag that you eat like this, because some people may think you are immature and don't know how to take care of yourself.

Just because you are a graduate and have a paycheck, it does not mean you need to start eating expensive foods.

▶ **Life Before Noon Tip**

Look for memberships to wholesale stores like Costco and Sam's Club. The benefits definitely outweigh the membership cost, and it gives you discounts to items other than food.

◇ Lesson 53 ◇
Credit Cards Are Your New Best Friend (And Worst Enemy)

It is easier to get a credit card in college then it is after graduation. Credit card companies are falling all over college students. If the credit card companies sign a soon to be college graduate up now, it means a lifetime of profit. Once you graduate, they won't be able to tell you apart from the high school drop-out working part-time at the local Blockbuster. While in college, you have potential. You must seize the moment!

Sign up for several different cards, just make sure they don't have annual fees. You need to start establishing credit so you can do things like buying a house in a couple of years. One of the major factors in your credit score is the length of time you have had credit. Another is the amount of credit you have available. So get as many cards as you can while you are young. It will pay benefits later as you get older.

Now that you have credit, what do you do with it? Use it but don't abuse it. Credit card offers open up the door to money flexibility. You can buy things now and pay them off later, but at much extra costs.

Almost everyone accumulates some credit card debt. With that being said, it can quickly get out of control and put you in a hole that is a bitch to climb out of. Use your credit card as a convenience but pay off the full balance each month. You will be building your credit rating while not saddling yourself with high interest expense. Save your credit availability for really important purchases, like a house.

At some point, trying to impress people in your drunken state, you will inevitably pull out the credit card and offer to pay the tab for the group. Most people will gather around you and cheer as the bar tab comes your way. There will also be some girls who take notice of this and assume that you have money and like to have a good time. That night is going to be a blast. The next morning will not be. You will take one look at the receipt and think, "Oh shit, what did I do?" Make this the exception, not the norm.

► Life Before Noon Tip

Look for a credit card that has 0 percent interest for the first year and then low APR after that. You don't want to get stuck with a great deal in the beginning and after the first year have it jump to 38 percent.

◇ **Lesson 54** ◇

Give Back To Your School

The first thing you will hear from your school after graduation will be "Congrats!" A close second will be "Let me give you some information on how to give back to your school." You most likely won't have any extra money, and if you do it will go toward bar tabs or meals. It is a good idea, however, to try and give some money back to your school. Most schools are nonprofit and use the money for scholarships and development. Donations allow schools to better their staff, which creates better departments. This ultimately leads to smarter graduates and better communities.

Being an active donor will open up opportunities for you that may not have immediate value but will down the roadwill. It could be a lead to a local alumni chapter that may provide contacts for prospective jobs or access to alumni tickets to sporting events. You don't have to take out a second mortgage to donate. Schools realize that finances for graduates are very tight, and they set up plans that can accommodate.

When we graduated we pledged to become a lifetime alumni members by donating $500. It sounds like a lot, but it was set up for payments over five years. That is only $25 a quarter, and we receive all the benefits. It is inevitable that they will continue to ask you for money, but it is likely that you will have a larger discretionary income the older you get. If nothing else, the hell that you raised in school is well worth a small financial obligation to make sure that future generations will be allowed to do the same.

College is not just an academic commitment. Being an active alumnus will open up years of opportunity. The benefit is having thousands of others out there willing to help you out just because you donate a couple bucks a month. Just do it.

▶ Life Before Noon Tip

List your alumni membership on resumes so potential employers can see that you are comfortable with networking and are connected socially.

Invest In Yourself

Although initially you won't have much discretionary income, it is still important to do something for yourself from time to time. Think of this as your personal stimulus. Work can get repetitive at some point, and you need to be able to break away and let loose on your own terms.

It is always easier to get through tough times when you have something to look forward to down the road. In college you have sporting events going on all the time, someone's big party coming up, or the usual favorite drink specials once a week. You want to have some fun things planned like this after college.

A great, cheap example is joining a recreational league. You don't have to be athletic at all. You can join competitive leagues if you want, or have fun on a kickball or cornhole (bean bag toss) team. Yes, that's correct, they actually have cornhole teams. Make it a point to schedule in time for activities like these because they can be easily overlooked. You should stay busy and want to be very involved at work, but if you don't have some release during the week it will end up affecting you negatively at work.

Another investment in yourself is your appearance. You don't need the nicest clothes, but you do need to be presentable. Clean, crisp clothes are essential for any office job. Even when you go out with co-workers you want to make sure to at least look respectable.

Be sure to invest some money in yourself and budget in some personal expenses. You want to have the availability to do fun, social things from time to time. If that means renting or buying a smaller place (that will be cheaper to cool and heat anyways) then that is totally fine. How much fun would it be to have a great place but not be able to afford going out?

▶ Life Before Noon Tip

Be sure to buy something new for yourself every couple of months. It can be something as simple as a shirt, or more expensive like a new pair of shoes. This way you can always rotate your wardrobe and won't be stuck with a big expense each year when it is time to buy new clothes.

Graduate From College...
And The Roller Skate Car

While a beat up 1980 Honda Celica with duck tape holding the fender up might be fine when you are in school, once you graduate you have to upgrade to something more respectable. The question is how far do you go?

Everyone has a dream car. Some want a big truck jacked up with huge tires while others dream of a fast, expensive sports car. Let's be frank. Your dream car is not going to happen right after college. Unless you are a Division 1 athlete who gets drafted, you won't have the money you need for those big purchases.

Be smart about things. Is driving an expensive car when you are 22 years old really that important? You are probably thinking about all the girls that will be impressed by it. Actually, girls will probably think you are driving you parent's car if you pull up in a brand new, loaded BMW. Plus, paying for it will leave nowhere in your budget for other things like going out. So, having a car too impressive will actually backfire on your social life.

You want a car that is relatively inexpensive but nice enough to at least be impressive. Instead of buying new, go for the 1 or 2 year-old certified used car from the dealership. That way you know that the car is in good shape and is still under warranty. Plus, car models stay the same for a couple of years so your used car is going to look just like a new car.

Priorities will change soon after college. Once you get through the fad of being on your own and having money, you will realize that certain things like status just aren't that important. Do yourself a favor and get a car that is acceptable to you and is not an eyesore. Cleaning your car and getting it checked on a regular basis will make just about any car look good.

► **Life Before Noon Tip**

Negotiate, negotiate, negotiate. Don't ever take the price on the window sticker as the final price. Also, don't think that any car is good enough to be a must-have. If you don't get the first one, a better one will probably come along.

You Don't Need A 50-Inch Plasma, Even If You Can Afford It

Budgeting will be the key to your happiness, especially in the beginning. How you handle your finances the first two or three years out of college will determine the next five to 10. Everyone is going to get in some financial trouble; the key is to limit how far deep you go.

Try to live like you did in college and get only the basics. You don't have to sleep on broken futons and survive off stealing food from college cafeterias, but it is a good idea to take things slowly. You have plenty of time to save up and buy things when they won't put you in a financial hole. Debt can be a very scary thing. There is acceptable debt, such as student loans, and there is unacceptable debt, such as credit cards filled with bar tabs and electronics.

Don't let debt limit your financial freedom. At some point it is going to be a wise decision to buy a place of your own. No one is going to lend you money if you have credit card debt that is nowhere near being paid off. Don't do things backwards. We promise it will be more enjoyable to own a new place that you have to slowly furnish than sitting 7 feet away from a 50-inch plasma in a 600-square-foot apartment.

◥ **Life Before Noon Tip**

Instead of spending money on an expensive television, budget yourself an allowance to go to the bar each weekend to watch the game. If nothing else, it is a great way to meet new people.

◇ Lesson 58 ◇

We Know It Sounds Weak But Balance Your Checkbook

Did you just cringe? "Balancing Your Checkbook" sounds like something your mom would tell you to do. Balancing your checkbook really means managing your cash so you have it when you need it. While you may make enough to cover all fixed expenses, you still need to keep track of how much money is available for your day-to-day spending.

While you might not think this is big deal now, trust us, you can take our word for it or learn the hard way. Eventually, you will be balancing your checkbook.

We are not saying that you have to break out the pencil and paper and write every purchase down. All you have to do is keep a simple Excel spreadsheet of each monthly bill and when it is due. Then log onto your online banking twice a week and make sure that you have enough to cover the bills. If you don't, things will go wrong quickly, here are two examples:

- You don't want to be out with a date when the waiter comes back to the table to explain that your debit card won't go through. How can this happen when your online account said that you had $100 left in your checking account as of yesterday? Easily. You forgot about the tickets you bought for Sunday's football game. The charge was pending when you overlooked it, and the charge finally went through last night. Now you look like a real winner as you take up your date's offer to pay. Lame is an understatement.

- How many stupid purchases can you possibly make time and time again. Balancing your own checkbook will make you review your wasteful spending. Once you realize how many 12-packs you have been buying, you will realize that it is more financially responsible to go with the 18-pack or case.

⚑ Life Before Noon Tip

Look at your spending habits and list them in order by necessity. Now, look at the ones on the bottom of that list and see if you can do without them. If so, try and save that money or add it to something at the top of the list and make that experience even better.

Write Your Personal Budget Down

The best way to understand your personal budget is to actually look at the numbers instead of just talking about them. Looking at your budget in a format like that of Microsoft Office Excel is the easiest and most efficient way to determine how much money is actually available.

First, determine how much money you will net with each paycheck. Secondly, determine what exactly your paycheck goes toward. Some of the most common topics are housing, debt, transportation, savings, and miscellaneous.

Once you have decided on your topics, all you need to do is determine how much money goes towards each one. Using a spreadsheet allows you to easily manipulate numbers as things change. Use your starting number for each formula and the changes will be simple. Below is an example of topics and what percentages are appropriate. These will be different for each person, but this will provide a starting point.

- ✓ Housing (rental/owned): 30%
- ✓ Debt (student loans, credit card): 15%
- ✓ Transportation (car, bus,): 15%
- ✓ Bills (insurance, electric, water, cable): 10%
- ✓ Savings (monthly savings, insurance: 10%
- ✓ Misc (drinking, eating out): 20%

When you start making more money, recalculate your budget. Be sure to increase your savings and/or 401(K) contribution with each pay increase.

▶ **Life Before Noon Tip**

Use a spreadsheet to layout all of your personal budget. This way you can change percentages as needed to determine where more money needs to be allocated.

◇ Lesson 60 ◇

Start Saving A Tiny Bit But Don't Tell Anyone

There is going to be no easier time to save than now. At some point a family or other responsibilities will consume most of your paycheck. It will be easy to justify not saving because of too many expenses. Get yourself in the habit now of putting a little bit of each paycheck into savings.

In the beginning, you can't look at your savings to support you if you are out of a job. Your savings will not be much because you can only put aside a tiny bit from each paycheck. Any amount of money you can save is a positive thing. It doesn't matter if it is $10 or $100 a paycheck, be happy with what you can contribute. The point is not to build your savings into hundreds of thousands of dollars, although that would be nice. The point is to get into the good habit of forcing yourself to save money.

A 401(K) is a great benefit to utilize if your company extends the offer. A 401(K) allows you to contribute money tax-free into a retirement account. Contributing to a 401(K) is generally easier than saving on your own because it comes out of your paycheck automatically. This way you won't miss the money because it never hits your net paycheck. Plus, most companies offer to match your contribution up to a certain percentage. Note to self: if anyone offers free money, TAKE IT!!!

Down the road, savings will become more important and may actually serve as your family income if something unfortunate does happen. You don't want to begin saving when you have to, because it will be a tough lesson to learn. Do yourself a favor and learn to put a little bit of money away with each paycheck so when you actually do need to depend on it you will already have a head start.

Finally, don't brag about your savings. Keep it to yourself. Don't mention to anyone that you have $5,000 stored away for a rainy day. If you do, people will always be asking you for loans, and your girlfriend will wonder why you don't spend the money on her. Also, other people will expect you to always pay for everything just because they know you have it.

▶ Life Before Noon Tip

> *Save money with each paycheck. It may not amount to much, but if you are planning a trip in the near future, you can use some of your savings to help offset the cost and keep the credit card balance low.*

◇ 7 ◇

SOCIAL LIFE
HANGOVERS HURT MORE THAN THEY USED TO

Pay attention to the differences of social life after college. College parties were some of the best times you can recall (or can't recall, depending on how much fun you had). You don't have to completely straighten up but understand that you are with a new group now and you have to represent yourself differently. Your co-worker may enjoy a chugging contest, but your boss might not want to funnel.

✓ Lesson 61: Party Behaviors Will Be Changing...For The Better
✓ Lesson 62: Throwing Parties
✓ Lesson 63: Don't Be That Guy Who Never Leaves The House
✓ Lesson 64: Establish Your Neighborhood Bar
✓ Lesson 65: You Don't Have To Stay Until The Bar Closes Anymore
✓ Lesson 66: Hanging Out With Friends Versus Acquaintances
✓ Lesson 67: Don't Be The Drunken Fool
✓ Lesson 68: Attending Sporting Events
✓ Lesson 69: Be Smart, A DUI Can Derail Your Life
✓ Lesson 70: Spend Time By Yourself

Party Behaviors Will Be Changing... For The Better

Everyone is going to tell you, "You need to start acting like a grown up; you can't party like you did in college." You don't have to change all of your ways. Actually, as long as you produce in the office and stay out of trouble, most people will like the aura of a younger person. There is also something to be said about representing young people. Take pride in having graduated and in your new responsibility. Older people who try to act immature and young come off as idiots. Young people who bring a mature but fun-loving attitude to work are assets. Take advantage of this while you can.

Some of the things that were your favorites in college will quickly grow old in your post-college life. You don't have to stop taking shots completely, but the days of double digit shots will be dwindling down. There are still going to be blowout nights, and that is a good thing. It is good to revert back to college days (think Frank the Tank) occasionally, but just try to plan for it so you can schedule things at work accordingly.

Another thing that will be changing along with behavior is choices. Don't get me wrong, you are still going to make poor choices and you will continue to learn from them, but some things that may have been "no big deal" because you were in college will become big deals now. Your friends may not judge you because they are in the same boat and have known you long enough. However, co-workers and bosses will be judging you and trying to get a read on you. Things like driving home wasted from the company function will not fly because 1) It is dumb as hell, and 2) You are now a liability to the company.

Have fun and drink along with the others, but act responsibly. It will show discipline and good judgment. Even better, meet with the group for some social drinks and then head out to meet your buddies to get wasted with the old gang. Be smart about things now. You may get to the point where you feel comfortable with a couple of co-workers or bosses and go out with a smaller group for drinks. When you are in a large, social situation...don't be that guy.

▶ Life Before Noon Tip

Make sure to have a favorite drink besides beer. This will allow you to drink socially with groups who may prefer one over the other.

Throwing Parties

One of the great advantages of college has got to be throwing a party for no particular reason. This is a must for everyone. Enjoy this while you can, because it will be a bit different after college. College is a time to let loose and enjoy your friends. After college you will throw parties for co-workers to help boost team morale and expand your social network.

Before you even think about throwing a party after college, you need to think "why." Why do you want to tear up your house and worry about people messing up your stuff? Before, you lived in a crappy college rental that you did not care about, because you knew you were out by the end of the year. Now you are going to live in the same place for a couple of years, so you really want to make sure your place can withstand it.

After college, most of your parties won't be random. You need to have a theme. Nobody wants to head over to your place to just sit on your couch and play drinking games anymore. Base your parties around televised sporting events like the football playoffs or pay-per-view Ultimate Fighting Championships. That way there is a reason for people to show up and something to center the night around.

Another difference to throwing parties after college is that people will actually show up with booze, beer, wine, and food. In college, people just go to a party and expect to drink for free. You will be pleasantly surprised that most people will at least bring a bottle of wine anytime they come over.

In college, random guys would show up at your party. Most of the time you wanted them out, because you didn't know them and you didn't want them mooching your beer or hitting on your women. After college, you will actually want people you are not as close with to show up. They may be a friend of a friend of a friend, but at least you have something in common, and you can extend your social network. So, be a good host and talk to anybody new as soon as they come through the door. Treat them as if you already know them as a friend, and they'll do the same.

▶ Life Before Noon Tip

> *Don't waste money on expensive kegs. When you pick up your keg of Natural Light at the store, be sure to snag a plastic topper from a different keg and leave it on the keg at your party. After three beers no one will be able to tell the difference.*

Don't Be That Guy Who Never Leaves The House

While most people will experience throwing a party in college we are willing to bet that all people will experience going out to a bar or someone else's party. As nice as it is to be at your own house, use your own toilet, and have your own room, it is important to expand your social horizon and enjoy a night out. Once you are working be sure to continue going out to parties thrown by co-workers. It won't look good if you only want to hang out when people go to your house and do what you want to do. Also, the invitations will stop coming if co-workers know you are only going to turn them down.

Bars are obviously a great meeting place, but other people's parties are great ways to make new friends. While your party is going to have a crowd of mostly your friends, someone else's party will include many people you don't know. You can have a great time partying and meet someone who may be able to help you with a work-related issue or score you tickets to the next sold out game.

The other clear advantage of going to co-workers' parties is to meet girls. A girl is much more trusting of a guy she meets at someone's party versus one she meets in the bar. At the bar there is a good chance that she is going to think you are a creep, but at a party of a mutual friend she will know that you have to be at least halfway decent or else you wouldn't have been invited. So let's review what we know about friends' house parties: makes work easier, not as much clean up, possible ticket connection, and a better chance of meeting girls!

▶ **Life Before Noon Tip**

As long as your aren't driving, always have a pre-drink at your house whenever possible. This way you can save money and show up at the bar or party with a nice buzz.

Establish Your Neighborhood Bar

You certainly spent some memorable days and/or nights at your favorite local college bar. We are confident in saying there is not a single college without a local bar. If there is, please feel free to let me know so we can be sure not to recommend it to anyone.

The bar was great because everyone would meet up there, you knew all the bartenders, and you didn't have a single care in the world. Everyone had something in common and that added to the fun. After you graduate you won't have that because you will have a job and real responsibility. Right? Wrong!

Yes, you have a job, but so does everyone else. That is what you have in common. You can still enjoy some nights at the bar and watch the game with buddies, because they too won't want to always close the bar down because they need to be at work early as well. Having a local bar is great because it is close to the house, and you can become familiar with the staff. You will be able to reap the same benefits you did in college.

There is something to be said for going to a bar and having someone toss you your favorite beer versus going to a bar and not being sure where to sit or what is on draft. Establish your local bar and rest assured that the other adults there have the same thing in mind. Drink some beers, have fun, watch the game, and head home.

Of course, there are going to be those nights that turn into all-nighters. Make sure you establish yourself at work as someone who is reliable, and don't plan on calling out sick. Plan those out ahead of time and schedule the day off so you don't look like a jackass. Keep going back to your local bar, and they will treat you like a VIP. It doesn't have to be the nicest or most popular place. Go somewhere you are comfortable and can have fun. A fun and comfortable bar will turn anyone into a fan. Think of your favorite bar in college, and we bet it was not the nicest of places.

▶ Life Before Noon Tip

Always over-tip at your favorite bar. You will end up saving in the long run with free drinks or superior service (plus, they deserve the extra tip because they are sure to get stiffed by at least one person throughout the day.)

You Don't Have To Stay Until The Bar Closes Anymore

While in college, there is a need to stay out until it is all over. You are afraid you are going to "miss" something classic like having the cops who are shutting down the bar allow you and your friends to take turns on the Breathalyzer to see who is the most hammered. Maybe you hang out to avoid looking like a lightweight or because you don't want to miss out on an easy hook-up.

After college, there won't be that need to close down the bar. Actually, it will be the opposite. You will want to leave at a decent time because you know that you have a long day at work to look forward to or an important meeting. This epiphany will not hit you the first couple of times. It is going to take painful hangovers at work, in which it appears the clock is actually moving backwards like in a high school history class, or making the inevitable boneheaded move and actually calling out "sick" because you got too wasted the night before. Either way, do yourself a favor and learn from the mistake.

A trick to do this is to say that you have to meet a friend of the family at another place around town. You won't lose face when you leave, and you just go home after that. Another option is to wean yourself off shots. Shots are the main reason for any hangover, and they are always way too expensive. You can drink 15 beers and not feel half as bad as four beers and three shots. Shots are fun because you get hammered so quickly, but adults who go to bars after work aren't looking for that. They want to have a couple of drinks and complain about their job or how annoying their wife is. Save the excessive shots for those once-in-a-while-meet-up-with-all-the-guys-at-the-stripclub-I-mean-bar nights.

You can find the nickel beer deals anywhere, but when work starts at 8 a.m. you won't want to be feeling like someone smashed a beer bottle over your head just to see if it would break. You have to be on your A game at work. Other people at the bar have jobs, too, so you won't be the only one ducking out early.

▶ **Life Before Noon Tip**

Drink a couple of glasses of water throughout the night. It will drastically reduce the hangover in the morning.

◇ Lesson 66 ◇
Hanging Out With Friends Versus Acquaintances

Many people will move back home after college as they are starting their professional life. This is a time to meet up with old buddies who stayed home and began work right after high school instead of going to college. These guys were probably in good shape after high school, because they were making money while you were in a classroom, but their jobs may not seem so glamorous now. Most of it will start out pretty harmless, but it might not be as fun as it used to be.

People who did not go to college did not have a chance to mature through the experience. The occasional fight or argument probably wasn't too big of a deal in high school, but you are in your early 20s and ready to start your career. You don't have time for drunken nonsense, and you may not have time for old acquaintances. If you haven't seen them in a while, you probably aren't that good of friends to begin with.

You have matured through college, and your values have changed. If someone has never moved on and has not gone through the maturation process then their values probably haven't changed much. They probably still think the tough-guy mentality is cool. Don't let any of your hard work be undone. Everyone who decides not to attend or finish college is NOT a bad or immature person. There are plenty of people who have reasons for not going to college, and they turn out great. Just be sure not to fall back into old habits by hanging out with certain people who are still looking for trouble. Not only did these people miss out on the academic side, they also missed out on the social side.

▶ Life Before Noon Tip

If you haven't talked to them in four years, they can't be too good of a friend. If they don't make you a better person, they probably aren't worth hanging out with.

◇ Lesson 67 ◇

Don't Be The Drunken Fool

It is easy to read this and think to yourself how you will never sell out and that you are going to continue to do things the same way you have always done them. It worked fine for you in college and even made you a popular guy to be around because of how much fun you were. Don't think of this lesson as us trying to tell you how to act.

The point of this lesson is that, like it or not, you are going to be surrounded by professionals of some sort. Depending on the size of your company, it may be likely that you run into a co-worker or vendor from time to time. No longer are you representing just yourself. You are now a walking billboard for your company. Do you really want to see a client, co-worker or vendor as you round the corner of the bar on the straight away of your naked lap?

Be smart about how you act. When you are in the local dive bar with five total people including the bartender and the guy passed out in the corner, then feel free to get as crazy as you want. Just don't do it in a random bar when you have no idea who is around. Even though something happens outside of work, you can still be held liable. Companies can terminate people if they are a poor representation of their standards.

Have as much fun as you can possibly have; just use good judgment. There is a time and place for everything. Even after college, sometimes naked laps or group shotguns just have to happen. Limit them to places where you feel comfortable, and you know there aren't going to be repercussions.

► **Life Before Noon Tip**

> *Don't invite your crazy friends to the bar where you know your co-workers hang out. Keep those gatherings to the bars where you know things can get crazy, and no one will care.*

Attending Sporting Events

In school, too many people took sporting events for granted. The tickets were cheap or free, but students were more concerned with tailgating or after parties. You probably fell into this category for most games, but there were a couple rivalries each year that everyone took seriously. After college, sporting events with bosses or co-workers will serve as a time for people to let loose and party as a group with excitement before the big game!

Sporting events are a great place to party with your friends and meet people outside of your circle. It is one of the few times where you will have an overwhelming similarity to thousands of strangers. Take advantage of it and enjoy the party. Anytime that you can network with people in a socially fun environment should be taken advantage of. There will be plenty of networking events in your career that, although productive, are going to bore you out of your mind.

▶ **Life Before Noon Tip**

If you are going to have people over for tailgating be sure to start at least three hours early and buy more beer than you plan on drinking. Stragglers will always stop by, and you will still be drinking after the game. Make your tailgate the one that people want to always attend.

Be Smart, A DUI Can Derail Your Life

Drinking and driving is not a smart idea. Anyone who enjoys drinking has probably, at one point or another, gotten behind the wheel of a car after having a few. Even going out to eat and having a beer or glass of wine can get you in trouble. Most people will say the easiest thing to do is not to drink, but there is no fun in that. Plus, you know you have to have a couple of drinks just to deal with some people in the group. With that being said, if you do plan on drinking when you go out, be smart about it.

A fun option to stay off the streets is to get a cheap hotel room. This way you won't have to end your party when the bars close. Hotels are a great place for people to freshen up after work or to meet up and pre-drink before meeting everyone else at the bar. The other obvious advantage is that you have some place close to take a consenting adult of the opposite sex back to (or in most cases, the hotel room will serve as a comfortable floor for your buddies to pass out on.) You may even be able to get them to help pay for the room.

If you plan on hanging out at bars that are close to your residence, but still too far to walk to, then see what transportation is available. Many places have a local "free" taxi service within a certain mileage. They basically work for tips and travel within three to five miles of the bars. If you live near the bars then these people will become your best friends. If not, then have a group meet at someone's house and share a taxi.

Don't plan on taking turns with a sober driver. No one will want to stay sober at the bar. One of the most annoying things is being sober in a drunken environment. Plan on everyone having fun and getting drunk. Just be smart about transportation because once it is out of the equation, you can party as much as you want without the biggest worry of a DUI.

▶ Life Before Noon Tip

> *Program the phone number of a local taxi service into your phone. When you go out for the occasional bender you will be way too wasted at the end of the night to try and remember the phone number. Also, always where a seat belt!*

Spend Time By Yourself

You are rarely by yourself in school. Most people live with roommates, study in groups, and don't do anything without their buddies right next to them. It is a big shock when you graduate, and you are living by yourself, alone.

Start now and take some time for yourself. Even if it is 10 minutes a day, make time to have a mental catch up or just think about the day ahead. You need the practice and the mindset. Being lonely and bored is quite different than choosing to be by yourself. It can be a bit depressing if you think you are stuck at home while everyone is having fun. Realize that it is healthy to do some things by yourself, and you can actually get a lot done. You also may find a couple of new hobbies.

Spending time by yourself is also a great time to get things done around the house without having it pile up. One of the most annoying things about living in a residence that you actually CARE about keeping clean is the chores pile up. Weekends are your time to have fun and get away from the work place. Don't let them be ruined by cramming a week's worth of tasks into two days. Allow yourself a night or two each week to move at your own pace.

"It's good for the soul when there's not a soul in sight"
- Dave Matthews Band

▶ **Life Before Noon Tip**

Use time spent walking to class or driving to work to reflect on your day or plans for the week ahead.

◇ **8** ◇

HOUSING AFTER COLLEGE
YOU DON'T HAVE TO SHARE A DORM

Learn to live like a king on a pauper's pay. Rest easy by following these simple steps to finding, furnishing, and paying for your first place. The most important things about your first house won't be material things. Choose a location convenient for you and also convenient for others to visit. Learn how to get things for cheap and the best ways to upgrade as needed.

- ✓ Lesson 71: You Have To Move Out Of Your College Town
- ✓ Lesson 72: Temporarily Living At Home Does Not Equal Failure
- ✓ Lesson 73: Find A Roommate Who Won't Drive You Crazy
- ✓ Lesson 74: Location, Location, Location
- ✓ Lesson 75: Renting Vs. Buying
- ✓ Lesson 76: A Picture Frame On A Keg Shell No Longer Counts As A Coffee Table
- ✓ Lesson 77: Make Moving Simple And Easy
- ✓ Lesson 78: Your First Place Does Not Need To Be A Palace
- ✓ Lesson 79: It's OK To Decorate Your House
- ✓ Lesson 80: Respect Your Surroundings

You Have To Move Out Of Your College Town

We know you love your college town. You dream of working a good job but still continuing to party at all your favorite bars. The college town brings you gamedays, friends, sorority girls, cheap living, and no worries. With all of that, it is so easy to try to prolong your college life after graduation. While it is tempting, staying in your college town is one of the worst decisions you can make.

One of the great things about graduating is the memories. If you stay, you'll have no perspective for what you have and you'll take it for granted, or worse, run thin the memory into nothingness. All your amazing college memories will drift away as you start working a normal job.

Also, if you stay, you never get out of college "mode." Since you are comfortable with your surroundings, you won't get excited or invigorated about something new. You won't make the effort to be adventurous. You'll keep dressing as you are comfortable.

Worst of all, at some point your friends are going to leave. You might be able to pull it off and get new college friends for a year or two, but before you know it you'll hit 40 and students are going to be looking at you like you are the old strange guy who keeps trying to come to their keg party.

Most of your time in college was spent partying, and that is what will continue if you remain. Let's face it, college is the best four, five or in some cases, six-year vacation you will have. Staying in your college town will make it challenging to get out of that vacation-mode and transition to the 40-hour work week. Plus, you'll need to be accountable for the lag between graduation and employment. Don't mess up your chances for a good job because you wanted to waste time after graduation. It will end up being a longer "vacation" than you intended.

▶ **Life Before Noon Tip**

If you are going to take extra courses towards another degree, then it is perfectly fine to stay where you are. Just don't do it because you don't think you are ready to move on. You have spent the past 20-some years figuring out what you want to do; time to go for it.

◇ **Lesson 72** ◇

Temporarily Living At Home Does Not Equal Failure

Most people go to school to get as far away from home as possible. As weird as it may sound, it is smart to move back home right after graduation.

Living at home with your parents is a great way to save money as long as it isn't for an extended time. You have a year window that it is socially acceptable. Think about it; even living at home for only your first three months of work will allow you to save at least a couple thousand dollars of rent and utility payments. That is not to mention all the free food. The time at home will also serve as a trial period so you can be sure that your budget is accurate and you can afford all of the bills.

Another great benefit of starting out at home is that it allows you to fully research the best available housing for you. That perfect apartment for you may not be available when you graduate. When you are at home, you won't be desperate to grab the first place you see. You will have time to acces all the options.

Don't worry about moving back in with your parents and how difficult it will be. They will understand that you are an adult now, and they will know your focus is in the right direction because of the hard work you showed while getting through school. Take advantage of all the things that come your way. This will pay off in the long run and also give your parents some much appreciated "togetherness" before you officially become independent.

▶ **Life Before Noon Tip**

> *Living at home may also help score some free things. If your parents see how hard you are working then they may choose to reward you with some financial assistance. If nothing else, they may help you out with some expenses just to get you out of the house quicker.*

Find A Roommate
Who Won't Drive You Crazy

You will probably have to take a roommate for your first place. This is a good thing, not a bad thing. Not only will it cut down on expenses, but it will also allow you to carry on some of your college living. Even if you can afford to get a place by yourself, it is a good idea to start out with a roommate. You can save money to blow on booze instead of rent. Plus, you also elongate the experience of living with a friend, because the next roommate you have will probably be your spouse.

Now that you want a roommate, do you go with someone you know or a random? While picking a random roommate is a great way to meet new people, it usually leads to a brutally cold relationship that ends with someone bailing and the other getting stuck with bills that are way more expensive than previously budgeted.

When in doubt, plan on moving in with someone you met at school. This will help you avoid slipping back into ways of old with high school buddies who never went to school and now have their names tattooed in Old English on their necks.

One thing you may want to stay away from, if possible, is finding a roommate at work. Living with someone and working with them can turn negative quickly. You want to be able to use work as time away from your roommate so you both don't drive each other nuts.

Whatever you do, don't have a woman as your roommate. You might think that she will introduce you to all her hot friends or one night you and she might hit it off. It won't happen. Girls and guys are in completely different mindsets, and you two won't get along. Plus, any girl you are dating is going to be insanely jealous of a girl roommate, which will hurt your chances of a normal relationship.

▶ **Life Before Noon Tip**

> *Regardless of which path you choose to take, a surefire way to turn a roommate relationship sour is with chores. Figure out how you want to handle chores initially so you are both on the same page. It is easiest if both of you just clean up after yourselves. This way everyone is responsible for their own mess.*

Location, Location, Location

Once you decide to move into your own place you will want to make sure it is conveniently located. You can rank convenience by two categories: professional and social. You want to find a happy medium between the two. Don't be too far from work to the point where...

✓ You are filling up your car more than once a week. Underestimating gas expenses will put a huge dent in your budget and limit your social availability. Let's face it. If money becomes short, you won't be driving to work any less. It means you'll have to reduce your weekend budget.

✓ If you are running late it will end up being REALLY late. There are going to be days when traffic is an issue, and you don't want that to double your trip time. If your trip time is going to be doubled you would rather have it be 30 minutes instead of an hour.

✓ If you are called in unexpectedly, you don't want it to take you more than 45 minutes to get there. When there is an emergency you will want to be able to get ready and to work within an hour. Being available will let them know you are reliable which will give you some much needed job security.

You don't want to be too far away from the social scene to the point where...

✓ The price of gas may limit your social decisions. You don't want it to take half a tank just for a roundtrip to the bar.

✓ You don't have a local bar within five minutes. You want to be able to go grab a drink for no reason other than just because. It is a good way to meet people who live around you and also will give you a chance to meet the local bar tenders and become a regular at your bar.

✓ It takes you longer than 30 minutes to get to the main social scene. Every city has a popular strip of bars that is a great hang out. You don't need to be next door, but you do want to be close enough to where it is a quick, easy trip. You also don't want to be more than a 30 minute cab ride or else the fare will really start accumulating.

▶ **Life Before Noon Tip**

If you are going to live in a social scene, college bars will be easy access to meeting girls your age. Don't be afraid to venture away from cookie cutter apartments and try a smaller, unique complex.

Renting Vs. Buying

Either one of these options is not a bad idea. Renting is a good short term option. It will allow you to save some money and live cheaply for a little bit. Just don't make renting a permanent thing. While it does save you money each month, you are still spending money that is not providing you any return.

Renting is perfect if you are single and want to have a roommate for a while or if you are actively looking for a place to buy. In the long run, you are going to want to buy something that is both affordable and accommodating. Buying a house is a huge investment, but it is also almost inevitable. Take your time and make sure that you make the right decision.

While you are renting be sure to set aside a certain amount of money each month that will go towards a down payment. There are different websites you can visit that will allow you to plug in numbers and see what kind of payments you can expect each month. Be sure you can afford your mortgage. When you look at the figures, go ahead and add 5 percent as a cushion. If you aren't saving money each month while renting, then renting will become a permanent fixture and you won't be able to buy. Do yourself a favor and rent while you look for something to buy, but do it productively.

▶ **Life Before Noon Tip**

Before you decide on what apartment to rent, take a drive around the parking lot a couple of times and see what kinds of cars are parked outside. You don't want to live somewhere if you don't think you will get along with the other tenants. (For example, lots of Cadillacs with handicap mirror hangers may signal that the residents may not be thrilled about late-night partying and loud music.)

◇ Lesson 76 ◇

A Picture Frame On A Keg Shell No Longer Counts As A Coffee Table

Don't think that you need to deck your pad out in the latest and greatest fashion. Remember, money is tight. Furniture should be the last thing on your mind. Hand-me-downs are a must for any new house. Wait until you are married or a bachelor with at least five years of consistent work under your belt before you buy the state-of-the-art stainless steel appliances. Until then, nobody expects you to have nice things anyway.

Your last days in college are a great opportunity to gather most of your needed furniture. When the semester ends, take a look at who else is moving out because you can probably upgrade an item or two when others just want to dump their furniture. Stay away from dorms because most rooms are furnished or too small to really have anything of value. Your best bet for good furniture worth your while will be neighborhoods nearby where senior citizens live. If you have a choice, go for women's furniture since it will usually be in good shape.

With little money, you can easily outfit the following rooms...

- ✓ Bedroom: bed, dresser, television
- ✓ Living Room: comfy couch (comfort over looks), coffee table (end tables optional NOT necessary), television stand, television
- ✓ Guest room/office: bed or futon, computer desk
- ✓ Kitchen: a couple of used pots and pans, paper plates and plastic ware, microwave

If you have to buy, then rank them in order of necessity. A bed is more important than a La-Z-Boy. As time goes on, upgrade items one by one as you can afford it.

► **Life Before Noon Tip**

When thinking about what style to buy, always go "urban." That way you get away with painted cinder blocks as an entertainment center, no head panel on your bed, bare walls, and a few simple things. Plus the urban style gives you a good excuse to get rid of all the clutter you have accumulated over the years.

Make Moving Simple And Easy

The first step to moving is to designate the necessary things. Don't waste your time by packing up things you are just going to throw away once you reach your new destination. This will save you hassle and time. Most of your college furniture is probably not salvageable, but you probably can't afford new furniture either.

You always have the option of starting out with nothing and renting a furnished apartment. It may be a tad more expensive, but the furniture will be nicer than what you can afford. Factor in how much you will save in moving costs and you may break even or save a bit. It is also going to be nice when you decide to move out of that place, because you won't have the hassle of moving that furniture out. If you do go with a furnished place, save some money when you can so that you can eventually furnish a place of your own.

If you are moving in with a roommate, talk to him and decide who is bringing what, otherwise you will end up with two big entertainment centers in your living room. Outside of bedroom furnishings you should be able to split the rest of the house up. Some things aren't needed at first and they certainly don't need to match. Everyone out of college is going to be in the same boat so don't worry about the small things.

When in doubt, throw it out. If you haven't worn that yellow shirt in over six months, toss it. If you have a fake pirate sword that you're saving because you might use it next Halloween, dump it. That collection of DVDs you will never watch again, trash 'em. The less you have, the easier it is to move. Actually, even better than trashing unwanted items is to donate them to charity. It is socially responsible and can also be used as a tax write-off.

▶ **Life Before Noon Tip**

> *Renting a truck and getting everything moved in one day is well worth the money. It will be much more annoying to tie up an entire weekend with a hodge-podge of help.*

◊ Lesson 78 ◊

Your First Place Does
Not Need To Be A Palace

Your first place is exactly that...your first place. No one is going to expect anything nice. Your first car probably wasn't the best so don't try to outdo yourself on housing. Affordability should be a bigger concern.

Take your first couple of years to financially understand your obligations and capability. You will want to save as much money as possible because you won't have as much financial responsibility at this point. This does not mean to save, save, save and never go out. Still go out and enjoy yourself, but save what you can. At your financial convenience you can purchase nicer pieces of furniture or electronics to replace your old ones. This will help make your place look nicer and keep you out of unnecessary debt by not getting everything at once.

Wait until you are making more money to get the bigger house and the fancier car. Too many times people live beyond their means, and it ends up biting them in the ass because they keep crawling into debt. What good is a kick-ass house if you can't afford to run your air conditioner for more than five minutes at a time?

You also aren't going to want to party in your house like you did in college. It is funny, but the smallest things will upset you that you used to laugh about when others got mad. Your house will appear nicer than any college housing simply because you will keep it cleaner and take some pride in it knowing that your paycheck now goes towards paying it off.

▶ **Life Before Noon Tip**

Feel free to switch around furniture every once in a while. It will give the room a different feel and make old pieces of furniture feel newer.

It's OK To Decorate Your House

Everyone in college had at least one of these five things on their wall:

1) A poster of John Belushi from *Animal House*
2) A poster of drinking games
3) Pictures of some model/actress
4) A street sign
5) BBQ/ketchup stains (I moved into a house my junior year in college with three of my best friends from high school and somehow BBQ and ketchup ended up on the wall during our first party. Someone actually got pushed through a window as well, but they were not hurt. Ah, the memories...)

These are fun things to have and perfectly acceptable in college. After college, if you still want to sport these in your house then try to confine them to a particular room. Use the other rooms to decorate your house a bit more maturely. You don't need to have fancy paintings or flowered wallpaper, but you can keep things clean and somewhat organized.

While you probably don't care what your house looks like, the girls you date will. No girl wants to come over to a dirty, cockroach-infested house. On the same note, most girls also don't want to come over to a obsessively clean house with shrines of past girlfriends on the walls. Be aware of how you are decorating because what is acceptable in your eyes may not be acceptable in others.

Many guys take the attitude that it is their house and girls that don't like the decorating are probably lame anyways. That is a great attitude to have if you want to spend your weekends watching *The Goonies: Where Are they Now* special premiere on cable. Besides, would you really want to get in a relationship with a girl who has respect for a sloppy house? That means she doesn't respect herself either. You want to be in a relationship with a girl that is a neat freak instead of one that frames pictures of a bunch of random guys doing body shots off of her (We emphasize the word 'relationship.' One night stand, yes please; relationship and a burning sensation during urination afterwards, no thanks.)

▶ **Life Before Noon Tip**

> *A couple of simple, inexpensive rugs will go a long way in making a house come together. Plus, you can strategically position them to hide stains.*

Respect Your Surroundings

No matter where you decide to live after college, you will make it work. You will either live near work and have a short commute, or you will live near the bars and tack on an extra 15 minutes to and from work. If you can find a place that is convenient for both work and play then consider yourself very lucky and try not to screw it up.

Wherever it is you call home, respect your surroundings. If you live in a quiet neighborhood because it is convenient for work, try not to make a habit out of loud parties. Parties are great every once in a while, but drinking until 5 a.m. every weekend, people coming and going, and loud music will get old for your neighbors.

Make every effort to get to know your neighbors. Easy ways to get to do this and earn their respect will be to simply take care of your property. Even if you are only renting be sure to maintain the outside. If someone is trying to sell their place and yours looks like it truly is a college house with a plastic pool in the front yard, and you can see more plastic beer cups than grass, then it will bring down property value and your neighbors won't like you from the start.

Also, if you know your neighbors on a personal level you have the opportunity to let them know when you are planning a big party. Let them know there will be lots of people and to call you if there are any problems or if it gets too rowdy. This will go a long way and help you stop any issues before they progress to legal ones.

If you choose to live in a party area then understand you also accept the location. If someone decides to have a beer pong tournament on Thursday night and it goes on until 3 a.m., don't be that guy who calls the cops. Just go over and talk to them and let them know that they are keeping the entire neighborhood up.

Being in that environment probably means that you have a pretty good relationship with everyone so these conversations should be easy. If the partying continues and it is difficult to sleep, cowboy up and take some sleeping aid.

▶ Life Before Noon Tip

Don't call the cops unless you want to have enemies as neighbors.

◇ **9** ◇

RELATIONSHIPS
THEY WILL MAKE OR BREAK YOU

Don't let a significant other hold you back. On the same note, you should complement them as well. Relationships will affect you more than you think so be sure to choose wisely. Also, be sure to stay in touch with the gang from college and make an effort to do something every year. Staying in touch will not only be important for obvious party reasons, but the networking aspect will also benefit you. The first couple years after graduation are important for fostering relationships for the rest of your life.

- ✓ Lesson 81: Dump Your College Romance
- ✓ Lesson 82: Take Care Of Yourself Before You Start Taking Care Of Someone Else
- ✓ Lesson 83: In A Good Relationship: 1 + 1 = 3
- ✓ Lesson 84: Make Sure Your Woman Is On The Same Page
- ✓ Lesson 85: Don't Tap The Company Keg
- ✓ Lesson 86: Stay In Touch With Buddies
- ✓ Lesson 87: Plan An Annual Event With Your Old Friends
- ✓ Lesson 88: Turn Monday Into "Manday"
- ✓ Lesson 89: Make Friends In Every Department At Work
- ✓ Lesson 90: Spend Time With Your Family

Dump Your College Romance

Everyone went through some type of college romance. It may not be serious, but it will be enough to drive you crazy for at least a little bit. College is a great time to go out with different girls and not worry about getting into a serious relationship. However, if you do get into a serious relationship, can you really see it lasting after graduation?

If you had any troubles with her in college, what makes you think that those problems won't be tenfold after you graduate? Is your relationship really important enough to jeopardize your career? The odds of both of you finding ideal jobs in the same city are slim to none. Enjoy the relationship for what it is...a college romance. Dump her! We don't care how hot she is. It is time to start your life after college, and you can't do it with her.

Granted, there are some people who meet in college and live happily ever after, absolutely. We have seen it happen, and it is a great thing. Out of 100 friends, we can honestly say we only know of one couple still together (and they are married with a child and doing very well). That could mean your relationship has a 99 percent failure rate.

One of the greatest things about landing a job after graduation is your ability to date and actually have money to do so. Go with the odds and start fresh after graduation. There are plenty of great girls to meet after college. Don't limit yourself to the same girl unless you are 100 percent sure she is the one (again, odds are that she is not).

▶ **Life Before Noon Tip**

Think of college romance like a keg. When the keg is tapped, it is time to get a new one.

Take Care Of Yourself Before You Start Taking Care Of Someone Else

---

How can you possibly expect to take care of a girlfriend if you can't take care of yourself? Take some time to assess where you are at in life and use that time to adjust to your job. It is one thing to continue a college relationship with a girl who might have been the one waking up next to you on the floor, but it is a totally different thing to meet a girl after college who doesn't enjoy bar food at 10 a.m. The girl who didn't know you in college might think those stories are humorous, but that doesn't mean she wants you to resort to old ways.

Get yourself financially stable before getting into any serious post-college relationship. It will actually be easier to save money if you aren't in a relationship, so being single and saving money kind of goes hand in hand. The transition from college to career is not necessarily a difficult one, but it is one that has many challenges along the way. The better off you are as a person the better off your relationship will be.

Also, in the early parts of your career, you need to limit your commitments so you have extra time to get ahead. If your boss asks for volunteers to work the weekend, but you decline because there is no way your girlfriend will understand that you will miss Sunday brunch at her Granny's house, you just lost an opportunity to get ahead in your career.

You have to take care of yourself, establish yourself in your career, and save up a little money before you start concentrating on someone else. You owe it to yourself and her.

▶ **Life Before Noon Tip**

Your parents spent years and years raising you so you can live the best life possible. Give yourself a fulfilling life before you pass on the favor.

In A Good Relationship: 1 + 1 = 3

Don't be confused about the title of this chapter; we promise it is not some type of math question. In a relationship, the sum of the parts should be greater than the individuals alone. You should compliment the other and make each other better people.

In college you can think of many examples to prove this point. If instead of a relationship you were forming a beer pong team, you would want to make sure that she can sink the next shot and make your team better. This example might be a bit of a stretch, but you get the point.

Be sure that both sides of the relationship have something to contribute and that includes you. No woman will want to support a man who stays at home and plays video games for a living. On that same note, it will be hard for a guy who works his butt off to just hand money over to his wife who blows it all at the mall.

Take your time and find out exactly what you want before you try to assume what someone else wants. When you have extra money at the end of the month do you want to save it, buy something for yourself or buy something for her? Answering a few simple questions will let you know where you are and help you make a better relationship choice in the future. You know your decision will be right when you each compliment each other and enjoy time together more than being apart.

Remember, when a relationship works, it just clicks right from the start. If you start out with constant issues and differences, the relationship won't succeed in the long run. Many people waste many years of their life working on a relationship that does not have a chance. Don't force it. Move on.

▶ **Life Before Noon Tip**

If you don't feel like your significant other makes you a better person then you can probably find a better significant other.

◇ Lesson 84 ◇

Make Sure Your Woman Is On The Same Page

Women need to be proud of their significant others, so they sometimes focus on short term goals for you. Getting a higher paying job, getting a better car, etc... They compare you to their friends' boyfriends and want instant gratification of why you are better. What they don't understand is that you may have to rough it for a few years for it to pay off big time. So you might be saving because you have some new company you want to form, but your woman will be pushing you to buy a new couch or install hardwood floors. She won't understand why she has to sit on an old nasty couch when you have $10,000 in the bank.

Make sure your plans are very clear before getting married. If a girl is a certain way while you are dating then she is probably going to remain that way if you take the relationship further. Even if she says she will change expect that to be a bonus and don't count on it. Make sure that your plans are clear before getting too serious. She needs to understand why you do things a certain way, and you need to understand that if you plan to do something then you need to follow through with it.

Personal time is one big thing that can cause major headaches if not agreed upon beforehand. Let's say that after your day job you are working on a project that requires you to be on the computer. While it might be fine at first, she will most likely start complaining about how you are always on the computer, and you don't spend any time with her. She probably won't understand why unless you explain to her what and why you are doing it. If she knows there will be a payoff in the end, then she will probably not hassle you as much. In her mind, if you are taking time away from the relationship then it should be on something that will benefit the both of you in the long run. Be clear about how and why you are doing something.

▶ Life Before Noon Tip

If you know things are getting serious, have discussions about your expectations and make sure you both see eye to eye.

Relationships ◇ 101 ◇

Don't Tap The Company Keg

Following this simple piece of advice can pay off with huge dividends regarding the longevity of your career. It is too easy to lose focus and get caught up in an office romance. Let's face it, from Monday to Friday there are only 120 hours. Of those 120 hours you probably spend 40 of them sleeping and 50 of them working. That means that you spend more time during the week with co-workers than with significant others.

You have to stay on track and realize that the best way to accomplish goals is to keep business and pleasure separate. Work keeps you busy enough as it is. Why would you want to try and balance a relationship in the middle of work anyways? Even if it isn't always fair, perception is reality for co-workers. The first time you take the side of your office fling, even if it is the right side, co-workers are going to scream favoritism, and you will inadvertently be dividing the office.

To further prove our point, we have personally witnessed both sides of this debate. One of our very good friends met his wife at work, and they ended up being perfect together. We can honestly say that is the only successful story we have witnessed. We have seen 10 times as many people get fired or forced to transfer out of departments due to poor choices they made with co-workers. Flirting and having fun is one thing, but it is completely different to take it to the point of a relationship. When in doubt, keep things professional and keep relationships outside of work. Besides, do you really want to spend 24 hours a day and seven days a week with the same person?

You may not think it can happen to you, but in the office, it is the women that are the aggressive ones. They will flirt with you, tease you, dress incredibly sexy, and put you in situations that your man-loins are saying "yes, let's do this." Don't give in. It only leads to disaster. Women use their sexual being to get ahead in the corporate world. Once you hook up with her, she owns you.

► **Life Before Noon Tip**

Most bosses are not allowed to date someone who directly reports to them. Don't limit your chance for a promotion because you think the secretary is hot. Keep it a fantasy.

Stay In Touch With Buddies

This is one of the simplest yet most important lessons in the book. It is too easy to let important friendships slip away and be consumed with your day to day obligations. Make every effort possible to keep in touch with your college buddies. They were the ones that helped you get through a time when you were on your own and couldn't always fall back on parents or childhood friends. Much of who you are comes from your friends, so be proud of that and continue the relationship so you can also continue to grow and learn from them.

Now that the sentimental part of the lesson is finished, let's look at the fun side. How many times did you end up hammered with college buddies until the bar closed and had to walk five miles home? How many road trips started out with two guys and ended up with six of you squeezing into a conversion van that your buddy bought by selling the car his parents gave him for college?

The fun times don't have to end after college. As you grow up you are still going to be going through the same things and can help out each other. Instead of sorority girls, hangovers, and bad grades, you will be going through engagements, 3 a.m. baby feedings and financial troubles. By the time college rolls around most people are well on their way to being who they are going to be. The friendships you developed in college were because you chose them. They weren't forced upon you because your parents were friends or because you sat together in class. Enjoy them and let them grow as you do.

Keeping up with your buddies doesn't require long conversations on the phone. It can be a simple call or email. If you don't do it often you will drift out of friendship faster than you think.

▶ **Life Before Noon Tip**

Staying in touch with buddies can also lead to job connections you may not have had otherwise.

Plan An Annual Event
With Your Old Friends

Use the 'staying in touch with college buddies' lesson and take it one step further. Annual events are a must for any group of guys. The first couple years it might be financially difficult to get everyone together. So, all of you should take a trip to where one of the guys lives and crash at his place for the weekend.

After your group gets a couple of years of working and saving under their belt you can begin to expand your events. There is nothing better than getting the old gang together for a weekend of nonsense. It is a great way to blow off steam and catch up with everyone. It is sad how soon people start to grow apart once their priorities shift to work and family. You deserve to have fun together. Making it once a year gives you ample time to save a bit each month, so when the event rolls around you aren't trying to put everything on a credit card.

Golf is an easy trip to plan, but an even better trip is to plan it around a sporting event. Even if someone isn't interested in the particular sport they can at least enjoy all the festivities that surround it. Be sure to be fair to everyone and take turns choosing destinations. You don't necessarily have to take turns planning it because, let's face it, we all have friends who would let too many details fall through the crack. No matter how tough work or relationships are, your annual event is the one thing you can look forward to and know that in less than a year everyone will be together and causing trouble just like the old days.

Once you are in a serious female relationship, it might be hard to convince her that you are taking a vacation without her. Be sure to let her know early that you have been doing this annual event each year, and it is tradition that you go. Don't back down once, or you will probably never join your buddies ever again.

▶ **Life Before Noon Tip**

Be sure to plan your trip far enough in advance so everyone can schedule with work accordingly. Start throwing around ideas for next year on the last day of your annual event to get everyone excited about the next one.

◇ Lesson 88 ◇

Turn Monday Into "Manday"

This lesson can mean many different things to many different people. The route we are taking with this is a very simple one. Previous lessons talk about road trips, ball games, and golf outings with old college buddies, which are all important, but it is also important to spend time with your local friends as well

"Turn Monday into Manday" was as catchy a phrase as we could come up with to prove this point. Any day of the week will obviously work and it will come down to what works for the group. Use one day a week and turn it into a dart league, regular poker game, or center it on a weekly sporting event. The point is to establish a routine and look forward to it because it will help the boring parts of your week go faster.

It's best not to have it on a weekend because you are going to be looking forward to the weekend anyway. Pick a day that not only gives you a chance to let loose during the week but one that also breaks up the work week. Spending time with friends on a regular basis, outside of weekend boozing, will help keep things in perspective and give you the mentality that no matter what happens at least you have Manday coming up.

Make sure your significant other knows that your friends are a big part of your life. Encourage her to organize a girls' night out during Manday to avoid conflicts of alone time.

If you are having trouble figuring out how to establish a Manday, go to www.collegestateofmind.com for some ideas and a game plan.

⚑ **Life Before Noon Tip**

Take turns choosing what sport to center your night around. Try to learn something new about a sport you don't have much interest in.

Make Friends In Every Department At Work

Positive working relationships are going to make or break your success at work. When people are on your side then people go out of their way to help. If people aren't on your side then not only will they make life harder for you, but they will also set you up for failure. Remember this: some people can't make it on their own, so they can only get ahead by making someone else fail. In the corporate world, you don't want to be on the bad side of anybody, no matter how much you dislike them as a person.

Learn what other departments do and take an interest. This will help build a relationship, and it will also make you more valuable to the company. In every job you have, you will rely heavily on other departments. Different pieces have to come together to get the job done and depending on how well you work with others will depend on how quickly you achieve your goals.

The easiest place to start when building a relationship in the office is at lunch. Everyone is going to take at least a quick break for a meal and want to relax without thinking about work. It is easier to find some common ground socially than it is to find some common ground at work, especially if you are in separate departments. Once you have established a personal relationship people will be more trusting of you which will spill over into your professional field and help build your credibility.

▶ Life Before Noon Tip

> *The best managers are the problem-solvers who allow the department to run itself.*

Spend Time With Your Family

Having family dinners and spending time together at holidays may not have been high on your priority list when you were younger. In high school, it was probably a pain to get up early on the weekend to attend some family event when all you wanted was to sleep in after a long night. In college, you probably enjoyed seeing your family because that meant a free meal or groceries, but in the end all they did was put a damper on the best party weekend of the year.

Once you leave the one continuous keg stand that is college, you will realize the importance of family and you will start to value their support and advice. We already talked about how your relationship with your parents will change, but it will actually be your relationship with your whole family that changes. You are not dependent on your parents like you used to be and as you get older, they will be the ones who become more dependent on you.

Make sure that your family knows how much you appreciate them. They are the reason you have gotten where you are and will get you where you are going. On the same note, you are part of the reason for their success as well so the appreciation will be mutual. At least send birthday cards to immediate family members and make phone calls on big occasions. You may be surprised to learn that you will actually prefer to have family dinners, not only because the food is free but also because you enjoy the company.

▶ **Life Before Noon Tip**

If you live close enough to home, Sunday dinners are a good time to catch up with family and usually don't infringe on bar nights.

◇ 10 ◇

HELPFUL HINTS
DON'T OVERLOOK THE OBVIOUS

Take advantage of easy tips to make each day of your life simple and easy. Minimize time spent on meaningless things to improve your productive time throughout the day. Plan on spending the weekend participating in a beer pong tournament? Then get your chores done during the week. Saving money to upgrade your current 15-inch television? Then try to eat out a little less each week. Learn easy ways to improve the way you live.

✓ Lesson 91: You Are A Big Boy Now
✓ Lesson 92: Decisions Are Easier If Your Choices Are Limited
✓ Lesson 93: Don't Over-Commit Yourself
✓ Lesson 94: Don't Waste Your Weekend
✓ Lesson 95: Get Something Done Each Day
✓ Lesson 96: It Is OK To Shower And Shave Everyday
✓ Lesson 97: It Is OK To Stock The House
✓ Lesson 98: Movies To Learn From
✓ Lesson 99: Make Opportunities For Yourself
✓ Lesson 100: Respect Every Co-worker, And Yes, Everyone Is Your Co-Worker

You Are A Big Boy Now

My boss once told me about his son who broke his arm and had to go to the hospital. They were in the hospital room waiting for a doctor to come in when a nurse asked for his insurance card to get the paperwork started. Without knowing the difference, he handed her his AUTO insurance card...he was clueless.

The student health service will no longer suffice as your doctor's office and appointments won't be made once or twice a year when you visit home. It is your responsibility to take care of yourself now that you are a big boy. Get health insurance and schedule doctor visits, even if you have to pay for it.

Now that you are a big boy it's not cool to be sloppy anymore. It is no longer acceptable to have a "hair-off" with your buddies and see who can go longest without getting a haircut. Getting a haircut once a month does not mean you are being any less of an individual or conforming to society.

If you want to conduct business in the professional world then you have to fit the part. Just as shaved heads and braided goatees were acceptable in college, image is important in the corporate world where perception is reality. Your appearance is as important as the results you provide in the beginning.

It is also time to start taking care of your body's appearance. Now that you are in your 20s, your metabolism will slow down big time. That means that it will take longer for your body to process calories. So you have to cut out the 5 a.m. pizza and the trips to Taco Bell every day. One meal a day should at least have some vegetables in it (French fries do not count). No more than one meal a day should be deep fried.

Do big boy things like scheduling a trip to the dentist, joining a gym, and jogging after work. Don't spend your nights and weekends being lazy, once your body starts down the road of fatness, it will be tough for it to come back.

▶ **Life Before Noon Tip**

While we are saying that you need to take care of yourself, don't turn into a metro sexual. If you find yourself constantly tweezing your eye browns and clipping your toe nails, you are taking our advice a bit too far.

Decisions Are Easier If Your Choices Are Limited

Continue the theme of college simplicity after graduation, but do it with a twist. Instead of being simple by wearing the same thing to class all week, be simple by limiting choices and saving time.

You are not part of the fashion world so you don't need tons of clothes. Streamline your clothing options to make it quick and easy. Saving a couple of minutes here and there will add up and give you an extra buffer for unexpected traffic on your way to work.

Buy multiple pairs of the same kind of sock so no matter what two socks you pick out of your drawer, they will match. So much precious time is wasted in the morning searching for two socks that match. The socks should be plain, solid black or brown without fancy designs so they don't stand out.

Buy one pair of black dress shoes and one pair of brown dress shoes. Neither pair needs to have laces but they do need dark, rubber soles. They need to be comfortable so you can wear them all day, but nice enough to wear around the office and going out. Many girls are going to encourage you to buy fancy shoes from Gucci or Prada and remind you that "shoes make the man." They are basically saying that they can tell how rich a man is by his type of shoes. You don't want to date these types of gold digger girls anyway.

Make life easier and get an interchangeable black/brown belt. A belt with a buckle that doesn't stand out will do. You don't need an alligator belt or a belt with a fancy buckle. Keep it simple and save some money by only buying one belt.

These are three simple examples for clothes. The theme of "keep it simple" applies to more than clothes. It applies to every aspect of your life. The simpler you can keep things and limit your decisions, the easier and quicker it will be to navigate through life.

▶ **Life Before Noon Tip**

Buy wrinkle-free shirts so you don't have to waste time ironing.

◇ Lesson 93 ◇

Don't Over-Commit Yourself

You have big aspirations, but you can never find enough time to get them accomplished. As important as it is to stay socially active, it is of equal importance to not over-commit yourself to others. Not only will it cause you stress, but it will also upset others because you won't be able to honor all your commitments. You inevitably will have to bail on at least one group. Finding a healthy social balance will help you avoid unnecessary stress.

For example, if you have meetings on Monday, softball on Tuesday and a dart league on Thursday, when will get you things done? You can wait until the weekend to get everything done, but then you can't enjoy your time off and you take the risk of something coming up that consumes most of your weekend. Once again, you have brought unwarranted stress upon yourself.

Schedule some nights each week for yourself that allow you time to unwind and get things done on a leisurely schedule. Don't be afraid to say no to people if they ask you to participate in something that you know there is no time for, but explain to them why you can't hang out (even better, try to rotate some activities so you can spend time with everyone and maybe even find a new hobby).

▶ **Life Before Noon Tip**

When somebody asks you to do something socially, even if you know you are going to make it, don't fully commit. Tell them that you may be able to make it. So, if something comes up or if you don't feel like it after a long day of work, they won't be disappointed if you don't make it.

Don't Waste Your Weekend

Now that you are spending your time at work for nine to ten hours a day instead of class for three to four hours a day, your weekend will become much more valuable. Don't use your weekend as an opportunity to sleep until 3 p.m. and party until 3 a.m. Get yourself into a routine so you get enough sleep during the week and aren't worn down from work. Sleeping in on the weekends is perfectly fine, but if you are waking up for work at 7 a.m. during the week then reward yourself and sleep in until 9 a.m. on the weekend, not 3 p.m.

Fridays and Saturdays can still be party nights if you want, but it doesn't mean shutting down the bar and then tapping a keg at your place after. Use your weekends to get a couple of things done that aren't so easy to do during the week. Try to get most cleaning and laundry done throughout the week so the weekend is open for just a couple of chores or errands and plenty of relaxation.

This type of weekend will be much healthier for your work week. You no longer can use the week to sober up for the weekend. Relax on your weekend and it will result in a better, more efficient week of work. Don't think you can't have any fun; just realize that your new phase of life needs to have a balance between work and play. Get crazy on occasions when everyone gets back together, not every Friday and Saturday. It also doesn't hurt to save a little bit of money by not partying every weekend, all weekend.

If you have a crazy, drunk-filled night on Friday then do something chill on Saturday. Two crazy nights in a row will have you zonked out all day on Sunday. As you get older, it takes longer and longer to recover.

▶ Life Before Noon Tip

Try to get one thing productive done each weekend. You will be amazed how you feel on Monday when you only need to concentrate on work.

◊ Lesson 95 ◊

Get Something Done Each Day

Partying is not the only way to waste away your weekend. Chores will add up quickly now that you actually care what your place looks like and how your clothes smell. It was never a big deal to roll out of bed on Monday morning in the same clothes from the weekend and head to class. Try to do that in the workplace and it will probably be a short-lived career.

Don't let your list of chores pile up to be done on the weekend. Your weekend will be consumed with more work and it will be like you never even had a break. Don't work seven days a week. You are already working five days a week so just do a little bit each night when you come home. This will blend nicely into the philosophy of not wasting weekends. They are meant to be a release for you and not two days to see how much you can cram into them.

Getting things outside of work done nightly will help keep you on a schedule and leave few chores for the weekend. For example, if you know you are busy with some type of social group on Tuesdays and Thursdays then leave Wednesday for laundry. Try not to schedule things on Monday evenings because you may either be stuck at the office playing catch up from the weekend or out with your buddies for "Manday."

Remember, there is going to be plenty of downtime that you aren't used to. Take advantage of this time to get the things done that need to get done. This will give you a much needed sense of accomplishment and help you remember that although work is obviously important there are things of importance outside of work that need your attention too.

⚑ Life Before Noon Tip

Do one chore every other night during the week so when the weekend comes around you can relax and invite people over to a clean house. (For example, Monday – clean shower while you are in it, Wednesday – vacuum, Friday – clean kitchen.)

It Is OK To Shower And Shave Everyday

Hygiene is a word that you most likely haven't known the meaning of and probably just figured out how to spell. You probably could have started your own business in college of selling cologne if you could have bottled the heavenly scent of smoky bar and dirty keg bucket. Waking up in the morning and heading to class with the taste of last night's beverage and the smell of the bar bathroom used to be a badge of honor. Not anymore. You can only get away with that in college.

Regardless of what you did the night before, your boss will expect you to show up to work prepared both physically and mentally. Remember that perception is reality (you may be sick of reading about the recurring theme of 'perception is reality' but it is the truth. Remember, unlike your friends, you haven't known your co-workers since grade school so all they can judge you on is your current behavior and appearance.) If you show up to work sober and ready to go, but aren't clean shaven, then your co-workers will assume that you had a late night at the bar and won't be ready for the big meeting. Don't give people a chance to judge you incorrectly.

Even though you may think that you are just going to work, you are actually doing much more than that. You will be a representative of your company and serve as an example to fellow co-workers. Everyone whose path you cross will be affected by you in some way. Set a good example and look the part. There is nothing worse than running into a client or vendor on a bad day and knowing that they may be questioning why they are doing business with you. If you hired a stripper for a friend's bachelor party and she showed up hungover and with hairy legs, would you feel comfortable?

◣ **Life Before Noon Tip**

Once you start taking care of yourself you will actually notice other people who don't and think, "Doesn't he realize what he looks like?"

It Is OK To Stock The House

Alcohol and partying won't consume as much of your budget after graduation, plus you will actually be making money. Stock your house with groceries and other necessary items. You will still want to have a sufficient amount of beer on hand, but you can add something more than Ramen noodles and cheese sticks. You won't have a student union to take advantage of so you will need to start grocery shopping whether you like it or not.

Buying groceries does not have to be an expensive chore. Check out the local Sunday newspaper for some valuable coupons. Try to buy certain things only when they are on sale and compare prices with generic brands. Keep it simple with lunch meat and bread and other things like that. You aren't going to want to make a big meal every night after working all day. Leave yourself some simple, inexpensive options so that you can treat yourself to a nice meal once in a while, or better yet, treat someone else to a nice night out.

You will probably eat out for lunch at least a couple of times a week. Add that to a couple of fast food stops at night and it really starts to add up. See what other people at the office do and if packing a lunch is an option, then try to do that a couple of times a week. You can make some inexpensive meals Sunday night that will leave leftovers for a couple of lunches each week. Any money you can save will really add up, so be sure to take advantage of saving whenever possible.

► **Life Before Noon Tip**

You can still be picky with what you buy, but be sure to keep your house well stocked, especially with toilet paper. The days of using Burger King napkins as toilet paper are over.

Movies To Learn From

Boiler Room – Young stock traders taking advantage of the imperfections of the system. It perfects the "act as if" model, where if you act like someone, you will eventually turn into that person. For example, if you want to be a high level executive, put in the extra hours and make yourself the go-to guy. People will feed off your mindset and opportunities will present themselves.

Office Space – An office worker is bored out of his mind at work so he figures out a way to steal hundreds of thousands of dollars from the company. The plan goes awry and he ends up quitting his job, burning down their company's building, and working construction. Don't steal from the company. Any amount of money is not worth losing your job.

Cool Hand Luke - A classic movie with Paul Newman on a chain gang. This movie shows you have to be a "world shaker" by having your own individual beliefs while fitting into society. Plus, it will teach you how to push yourself and make yourself stand out in a crowd. You will remember the line, "What we have here is a failure to communicate."

Wall Street - Gordon Gekko played by Michael Douglas teaches you that "greed is good" and that some rules are made to be broken. You will see that once you achieve your first success, it is very easy to do it again.

Glengarry Glen Ross - All you need to watch is the first 30 minutes to see the speech from Alec Baldwin's character. The movie teaches you that while many of your co-workers have the same job title, you can still stand out. Work harder, smarter, and faster than everyone else, and you will rise to the top. Just remember, "coffee is for closers."

Caddyshack – Alright, there really isn't much to learn from this as far as being successful goes, but the movie is a classic. It should be watched as much as possible ("It's in the hole!")

▶ **Life Before Noon Tip**

> *Once you are in a relationship, your woman will want to watch romantic comedies more than the action movies. If you want to see an action flick, call one of your buddies and see it without your woman. On the same note, let her go see Sex and the City 2 with her girlfriends. Don't let her drag you to it.*

◇ Lesson 99 ◇

Make Opportunities For Yourself

Anyone who plans on accepting a job, working exactly eight hours a day, and sitting in an office with their door closed is going to be in for a rude awakening. What do you think it means when a company offers you a position? It means exactly what you read. It is simply a position, or better yet, a spot on the team. They are giving you an opportunity to get your foot in the door. What you do from there is up to you. Don't just ride the bench; step up and be a contributing player.

Every company absolutely needs workers that are not looking for advancement. These workers are on the front line and are completely satisfied with their current job duties and salary. They expect to work their complete shift, break for exactly one hour at lunch, and then clock out as soon as the shift ends. If you are reading this book then we are confident that although you might start at the bottom of the hierarchy, you expect to move up aggressively through your career.

Go out of your way to be noticed. Once you have people who directly report to you, make sure they know that you have an open door policy and that they can come see you for whatever and whenever. You will not have all the answers, but you should know who to get them from. Get involved with the company and volunteer yourself for projects that may not be directly related to you but that give you more insight into the bigger picture.

▶ Life Before Noon Tip

> *You might start thinking, "Why do I work so hard when my co-workers don't do crap and still make the same money?" Just remember, only the strong survive. A year from now you will be promoted and they will be looking for another job.*

◇ Lesson 100 ◇

Respect Every Co-Worker...And Yes, Everyone Is Your Co-Worker

This isn't a lesson in manners nor is it advice on how to heal the world and solve life's mysteries. This is simply a reminder that everyone needs to be shown the same respect that you expect to get from others. You know your company is a good one to work for when the president knows the names of many of his employees from top to bottom. If someone is not liked or does not care about his co-workers then who would possibly put him in charge of everything?

Think of successful leaders you know personally, and we bet their co-workers respect them. Legendary basketball coaches Bobby Knight and Coach K. (Michael Krzyzewski) have two vastly different coaching styles but their success is almost identical. Different people need to be managed different ways, but everyone needs to be respected the same. If someone does something so egregious to lose your respect then they probably need to also lose their job.

Once you start working be sure to take time to meet everyone. You are going to want vice presidents and upper-level management to know your name, but you also need to make sure people below you know who you are as well. Upper-level management will give you the tools to be successful, but they will not have any part in your actual success. The front line employees are the ones who execute. They are the ones you need to go out of your way for. When the people come to take out the trash don't act like you're too busy to say hello. They have a job to perform just like you. If someone from maintenance is trying to maneuver a ladder down a narrow hallway then put your coffee down, get up off your ass, and help him out. Why would you expect someone to go out of their way for you if you won't go out of your way for them?

▶ Life Before Noon Tip

Regardless of hierarchy, everyone has a job to do and is dependent on others. It sounds selfish when you really break down the Golden Rule of treating others as you would like to be treated, but it is absolutely necessary to follow if you want to be successful. If you work well with others and produce results, there will be a spot for you in any company!

KEG BUCKET LIST
THINGS YOU MUST DO BEFORE YOU BEGIN WORKING

You don't want to look back at your college years knowing that you did not do these things. You can't start your career without accomplishing the things on this list. This list is not the end all be all, but it is at least the minimum that needs to be done. You probably won't remember your GPA 10 years out of college, but we guarantee you will remember the one time at that party when....

- ✓ Take a road trip.

- ✓ Attend a random concert.

- ✓ Attend an athletic event that doesn't interest you.

- ✓ Close down a bar.

- ✓ Show up to a tailgate with a bottle of Boone's Farm.

- ✓ Get your most embarrassing moment out of the way (Everything else will seem easier).

- ✓ Construct a living room on your front lawn.

- ✓ Burn your college books and notes **AFTER** graduation.

- ✓ Learn the five fastest ways to drink a beer.

- ✓ Before your life has meaning, test death (sky dive, bungee jump).

- ✓ Crack open a beer first thing in the morning.

- ✓ **TELL US MORE OF YOUR FAVORITES AT** www.collegestateofmind.com.

About the Authors

Dan Gura certainly did his part to make sure that Florida State University ranked as one of the nation's top party schools during his tenure. His house served as party central and a walk to his favorite bar, The Palace, was a daily routine. He does not downplay the importance of academics, but his concepts rest on the importance of lessons learned outside of the classroom in everyday life. He earned his marketing degree from FSU and is now a marketing manager at one of the most successful casinos in the world.

David deMontmollin graduated from Clemson University and kept the college experience going at Arizona State University. As a star on Travel Channel's *American Casino* and co-author of *Las Vegas Little Black Book: A Guy's Guide to the Perfect Vegas Weekend*, David has been coaching guys how to play hard for a decade. His expertise has landed him numerous television and radio show appearances including ESPN's *Cold Pizza*, SpikeTV's *Casino Cinema*, *The Tom Leykis Show*, *The Adam Carrola Show*, and ESPN Radio's *The Herd*.

Special Thanks

We want to take a moment to thank all the people for helping us write this book. Some contributed ideas while others just stayed out of the way and allowed us to write which is equally important. Every story or odd comment in the book is actually true, so we have to give a big thanks to our friends who supplied most of the humor throughout the book. Thank you to those who served as "creative mentors" and showed us that you can be passionate about writing while still making the subject entertaining.

A very special thanks to our spouses (yes, surprisingly enough we are married), family, 421 Murat guys, the NFAs, the Booty Lounge crew, the Pasqbo Rawstle team, everyone at The Palace, Sloan Street Bar, high school and college friends, work friends old and new, friends around town, good musicians/actors, good sports writers, and anyone who we have ever drank a beer with.

And finally, thank you to our parents for being patient and helping us through college...four years flew by like a drunk Thursday night.

Made in the USA
San Bernardino, CA
14 December 2015